SCHOLASTIC

CANDIDATES, CAMPAIGNS & ELECTIONS

Projects ★ Activities ★ Literature Links

Linda Scher & Mary Oates Johnson

NEW YORK • TORONTO • LONDON • AUCKLAND • SYDNEY
MEXICO CITY • NEW DELHI • HONG KONG • BUENOS AIRES

Teaching *Resources*

Dedication

For Mary—the best of best friends

Editor: Mela Ottaiano
Cover design: Brian LaRossa
Interior design: Melinda Belter
Cover photograph ©tessroo/morguefile.com
Illustrations: Teresa Anderko; Drew Hires (maps)
Poster design: Melinda Belter

ISBN-13 978-0-545-03514-9
ISBN-10 0-545-03514-7

Contents

Introduction

Advertisers, sports announcers, and radio disc jockeys know that Americans love contests! Once every four years, our nation engages in the most important, hard-fought, hotly debated contest that a democracy ever holds—the presidential election. Yet only about half of the eligible voters actually take part in the contest by casting their vote for one of the candidates. And voter turnout is even lower during off-year elections when only local, state, and Congressional representatives are running for office.

Through the activities in *Candidates, Campaigns & Elections*, you can help students become active in the American political process. This book offers ideas to get students thinking, writing, and speaking about elections. They'll learn that elections are more than annoying sound bites and commercials on television. Elections are about real candidates and important issues. They're also about the process of campaigning, about using the media, and building support. By studying this process and engaging in it themselves, students will become more educated, informed citizens, able to play a part in our democratic system.

The pages that follow contain activities, games, information, handouts, and literature tie-ins for students of different ability levels and different learning styles. Students will learn the chronology of an election, the tricks to writing a good campaign speech, and some ways to analyze a speech for propaganda. They'll follow a candidate throughout an election, report on his or her campaign, and participate in a mock election.

Candidates, Campaigns & Elections is a flexible resource. You can pick and choose from the information and activities that you feel are the most appropriate for your class. Enjoy!

Using the Poster

The poster bound in the center of the book explains the presidential election process. If you are teaching an election unit during a presidential election season, be sure to refer to the poster as you and your students discuss the various points along the road to inauguration. You may want to add stick-on notes at certain points to indicate the outcomes of primaries, vice-presidential candidate selections, and the winners of the actual election.

Resources

Books for students

The Class Election From the Black Lagoon by Mike Thaler & Jared Lee (Scholastic, 2003)

Electing the President by Barbara Feinberg (Henry Holt & Company, 1995)

Elections in the United States by David Heath (Capstone Press, 1999)

Landslide! A Kid's Guide to the U.S. Elections by Dan Gutman (Aladdin Library, 2000)

The President: America's Leader by Mary Oates Johnson (Steck-Vaughn Company, 1996)

Presidential Elections and Other Cool Facts by Syl Sobel (Barron's Juveniles, 2000)

So You Want to Be President? by Judith St. George (Philomel Books, 2000)

The Voice of the People by Betsy and Guilio Maestro (Mulberry Books, 1998)

The Vote: Making Your Voice Heard by Linda Scher (Steck-Vaughn Company, 1993)

What Presidents Are Made Of by Hanoch Piven (Atheneum, July 2004)

A Woman for President: The Story of Victoria Woodhull by Kathleen Krull (Walker & Co., 2004)

Web sites

Special note: At the time this book went to press, the Web site addresses were correct. Please preview each site to make sure the material is suitable for the developmental level of your students.

Ben's Guide to U.S. Government for Kids
http://bensguide.gpo.gov
Named for Benjamin Franklin, this site provides extensive background on the federal elections and the election process.

CNN
http://www.cnn.com
A great place to find up-to-the-minute coverage of the 2008 presidential race.

Federal Elections Commission
http://www.fec.gov
The FEC is an independent regulatory agency created by the federal government to administer and enforce the laws that govern the financing of federal elections. Students may need your help to navigate this site, including its statistical data, but it's worth the effort. It includes loads of information on voter registration and turnout in recent elections.

Kids Voting
http://www.kidsvotingusa.org
A teacher-developed site that includes grade-appropriate activities ready for downloading, on-line activities for kids, and links to other election-related sites.

League of Women Voters
http://www.lwv.org
A good site to explore for information and tips on how to be a savvy voter.

National Student/Parent Mock Election
http://www.nationalmockelection.org
This Web site provides information on how to enroll in the next National Student/Parent Mock Election. In the 2004 event, more than four million votes were cast.

Project V.O.T.E.
http://www.sos.state.tex.us/elections/projectvote/
The office of the Texas Secretary of State provides a voter-education program for students.

Scholastic Election 2008
http://teacher.scholastic.com/scholasticnews/indepth/election2008/
At this site, students can submit questions for Scholastic's Kid Reporters to ask the candidates on the campaign trail. Also includes links to election-related *Scholastic News* articles.

Election Basics

What makes America work? In our more than 200-year-old democracy our success as a nation has much to do with the process by which we select our leaders. While in some countries today, the changing of leaders still takes place with civil unrest, this process has been a peaceful one in the United States since George Washington first took office. From the town meetings of New England to the mayoral and council meetings that heat up boroughs, parishes, and counties across America, we choose our leaders by voting and we do it in a sometimes intense but almost always peaceful and orderly way.

Americans choose their leaders in an exciting, multi-step process. Each step along the way, especially on the road to the White House, has its own special vocabulary. This section offers activities for understanding government and the election process and its basic vocabulary.

Getting Started

Your students probably know more about voting and elections than they realize. Many may have voted in class, at camp, or in clubs. Some students may have won elections—for student council, club offices, or camp monitors. Discuss ways students make "democratic" decisions at home (on movies and other recreational activities, where to eat or what to eat, what to watch on television or which radio station to listen to in the car, curfew or house rules), at school (student government, classroom activities), at after-school clubs or sports, and in social or religious organizations. Although many of the activities students name may not involve formal elections, they require many of the same decision-making skills students will use when they become voters.

After discussing students' personal experiences, ask them to tell what they know about local, state, and federal government elections.

KWL Chart

Conclude your discussion by making a KWL (What We **K**now, What We **W**ant to Learn, What We **L**earned) chart or bulletin board about elections. Have students list what they already know about elections in the first column. Write the questions that arise from your discussion in the middle column. Refer to the chart, adding and answering questions, as the class learns more about elections. Be sure to review the chart as you finish your election unit.

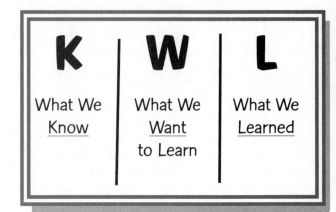

Building Background Knowledge

In order for students to get the most from the activities in this book—and eventually become knowledgeable participants in our democratic system—they should have some prior knowledge

Jigsaw Technique

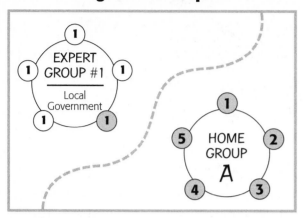

about our government. This process (see diagram above) will help students create some helpful common prior knowledge, and it will also put greater responsibility for learning on students themselves.

Divide the class into five groups of about equal size. Label the groups A, B, C, D, and E. Tell students these groups are their "home" groups. Within each home group, assign each member a number. For example, if you divide a class of 25 students into 5 groups, each group will have members 1, 2, 3, 4, and 5. Explain to students that they will work in different groups to become experts on one kind of government, such as local or state, or one branch of the federal government (executive, judicial, and legislative). Have all the students who have been assigned the number 1 work on becoming experts on local government, all those assigned number 2 become experts on state government, and so on, until all students are working in an expert group. After they've become experts, they will return to their home groups and share what they've learned.

Give each expert group a copy of Activity Page 36. Have students use books, magazines, newspapers, and the Internet to gather as much information as they can to answer the questions. They can also call or e-mail local government offices to find the answers to questions. Students should be prepared to share what they have learned with their groups both orally and visually using charts or posters they have prepared.

Words in the News

Have students brainstorm terms that they associate with the election process. (See the Election Terms below and the Glossary on page 39 at the end of the reproducible My Election Journal.) Make a master list of terms on the board. Write each term students have chosen on a large sheet of poster paper and hang them around the classroom. Have students bring in news articles using these terms and post them under the appropriate headings. Before posting their articles, students should underline key terms and summarize their articles for the class. Encourage students to use context clues to discover the meaning of the terms. Discuss the terms as a class so you are sure that students understand the meanings.

Election Terms

ballot: a printed or electronic form used in voting

direct mail: mass mailings sent by candidates and political parties to selected voters asking for support and money

endorse: to publicly support a candidate

executive: the government branch that enforces laws and is headed by the President

exit poll: a poll taken on Election Day as voters exit the polling place

incumbent: a person already holding a political office

judicial: the government branch that interprets laws and includes the Supreme Court

landslide: an overwhelming political victory

legislative: the branch of government that makes the laws and includes Congress

on one's coattails: benefiting from someone else's political popularity or success

opinion poll: a survey to find out what people think

polling place: a place to cast votes in an election

propaganda: a form of communication that tries to spread and promote a certain set of beliefs

recount: counting the ballots a second time because of a very close election

registration: signing up to vote by filling in your name and other information about yourself on a special form

runoff election: a second election held for an office when no candidate receives a majority of the votes in a general or special election. (A runoff election is between the two candidates who polled the most votes in the first election.)

sound bite: a fragment of television footage, usually nine or ten seconds long, especially one broadcast during a news report

Political "Jeopardy"

Invite students to play a game of Political "Jeopardy" using the vocabulary terms they pick up during their election study. To play, divide the class into small groups. Have each group make up a series of answers to questions that use students' vocabulary terms. For example:

ANSWER: Democratic Party
QUESTION: What is the name of a political party?

ANSWER: Elephant
QUESTION: What is the symbol of the Republican Party?

ANSWER: Denver
QUESTION: What is the location of the 2008 Democratic National Convention?

Since some answers may fit more than one question, you can be the final judge of correct answers.

Electionary

Play a game of Electionary using the cards on Activity Pages 37 and 38. Students can cut out the cards, color the backs, and then fold and tape the cards. (You may want to laminate them before use.) This game takes four players and all cards are dealt. Play goes in a circle with the first player pointing to a card in the hand of the person to his or her right. The player holding the card reads aloud the definition of the term on the card. If the player who has pointed to the card names the term correctly, he or she receives the card, which is placed to his or her side. If the player does not name the term correctly, he or she does not get the card. Play then continues clockwise around the circle with the next player pointing to a card in the hand of the person to his or her right. When a player has no cards, he or she is out of the game. The person with the most cards after four rounds of play wins. The game is more challenging if a timer is set before play begins and each round of play is completed within a specified time.

An Overview of the Electoral Process

Keeping Track With My Election Journal

The reproducible journal on Activity Pages 39–54 provides an interactive way for students to keep track of the events of the presidential campaign and election. They'll record information about the candidates, results of the primaries and caucuses, their thoughts about different stages in the election process, and more. You will find references to specific journal pages in several of the activities throughout this book.

First, to create a booklet, copy the 16 pages back to back, stack them in order, fold the stack in half, and staple the pages together at the fold. Hand out the journals and ask students to preview the pages to help them keep in mind the kind of information they'll need to look out for during their election study. Have students fill in pages Journal Pages 1–6, doing research as necessary, to access and/or build more background knowledge.

Finally, tap into students' creativity by encouraging them to paste in pictures found in magazines or newspapers, draw their own pictures, or color the illustrations throughout the book. As they fill in the pages, they will be creating a wonderful record of this presidential election.

A "Work in Progress"

If you are teaching an election unit during a presidential election year, this activity can become a "work in progress." Have students begin a mural or collage for the classroom illustrating each of the stages in the electoral process. Students should use original drawings as well as pictures from magazines, newspaper headlines, campaign banners, and bumper stickers to make their mural. Working in groups, students can illustrate a different section of the mural:

✔ Candidates announce

✔ Candidates campaign in Republican and Democratic primaries

✔ Major parties hold conventions

✔ Third party activities, if any

✔ Party nominees for President on the campaign trail

✔ Election Day

✔ And the winner is . . .

✔ Inauguration

Since some parts of the mural can be completed before others, this can be a work in progress with some groups planning their parts of the mural while others have already completed theirs. By inauguration time, your work in progress will be a classroom masterpiece!

It's Primary

Every race begins with the candidate's announcement that he or she is planning to run for office. In the race for President, candidates usually make their announcement at least one year and sometimes two years before Election Day. As candidates announce their intention to run for President, students can record the names on Journal Page 7.

The primary elections are the races that narrow the field. In these elections voters decide who their party's candidates will be. Many states have primaries in which all eligible voters can participate. Candidates who hope to win the race for President must enter primaries to win their party's nomination. Most presidential primaries take place between January and June of a presidential election year. Some of the earliest contests are in Iowa and New Hampshire. A big win in an early primary can help increase a candidate's momentum in raising funds and gaining the support of other elected officials in their political party.

The day in March when more state primaries are held than on any other day has been known as Super Tuesday since the 1980s. Beginning with

CAUCUS

Instead of primaries, a few states have caucuses attended by members of a political party. At this meeting, members select delegates to state or national nominating conventions. Sometimes the first round of caucuses takes place throughout the state in many different communities. At these meetings delegates also choose candidates to run for state and local elections.

the 2004 election year, however, the concept of Super Tuesday has been in flux. More states have been pushing up the dates of their contests. As this happens, there has been some concern that this kind of front-loading may have some negative effects. More is sure to be revealed over the course of this election year. This is a topic you can follow closely with your class.

Often, a candidate is an *incumbent*, or a person running for office who already holds that office. When that happens, members of the incumbent's own party are not as likely to put up a challenge. In most elections, the incumbent has an advantage. In elections where there is an incumbent trying for a second term as President, this person usually receives the political party's support and nomination.

In the 2008 election, there is no incumbent. Usually, as in this case, candidates from both parties have members of their own party challenging each other for the nomination. There are also usually two sets of primaries—one for Democrats and one for Republicans. A voter can cast a ballot in one primary or the other, but not in both. In primary elections candidates from the same party also compete for the chance to run for the Senate and the House of Representatives as well as for state and local offices.

Until the nominating conventions begin in midsummer, presidential candidates travel from state to state trying to convince voters that they are the best person for the job. By the time the conventions start, many candidates have run out of money or supporters and have dropped out. Only the strongest fundraisers and vote-getters remain.

Countdown to the Conventions: 2008

By completing Journal Pages 8–11, students can follow the top presidential hopefuls through the primary season. Students can fill in the results of their state's primary or caucus, along with those in the rest of the country. Encourage students to track how the race is going for their favorite candidates. They can find the results of each primary on television, in newspapers, and on the Internet, and then record these results in the proper column.

At the Races

Some weeks before primary season begins, on a large, heavy sheet of oak tag, create a long, circular race track to place on the bulletin board. Mark the track into 20 segments of roughly the same size. Clearly mark the starting and finish lines. Divide students into groups representing each of the candidates competing for President in both the Republican and Democratic presidential primaries. Have each group create a paper symbol to represent their candidate. Instead of making symbols, students may use newspaper or magazine faces of their candidates (glued to oak tag or laminated). Each group will be responsible for tracking its candidate's standing in the primary, using newspaper, Internet, and television reports. This activity works best if students follow at least 10 primaries over the course of the primary season. As candidates drop out, the date of their departure from the race should be noted on the track. Groups can advance their candidates along the track in the following order:

1. Candidate wins 60 percent or more of vote = 2 segments
2. Candidate wins 40 to 59 percent of vote = 1 segment
3. Candidate wins 20 to 39 percent of vote = 1/2 segment
4. Candidate wins less than 20 percent of vote = no movement

As students move their candidates around the track, they will find that a few never leave the starting gate, while others are stalled midway. Only a few get close to the finish line and only one wins the race.

DID YOU KNOW?

In many major American cities, the mayor is elected by less than 10 percent of those eligible to vote.

For the File

Every four years on Election Day voters pick a President and Vice President. But they also may be voting for members of the House of Representatives, the Senate, governor, and for local leaders. (See pages 6 and 7 for an activity that will help students gain an understanding of how local, state, and federal governments work.) If possible, distribute copies of a sample ballot. Have students find an example of a national race and a state race on the sample ballot.

Explain to students how ballots are marked in your community. In most places voters use optical scanning devices or mechanical or electronic voting machines with levers. In a few places, particularly rural areas in the Midwest, paper ballots are still used. While much of today's world is conducted online, the shift to a fully electronic voting system, or even a system that is a nationwide standard, has been slow. Some cities and towns that have tried electronic voting are beginning to question how safe it is and are advocating a return to paper ballots. There is concern that this type of system would be susceptible to tampering by computer hackers. Others worry that the machines may malfunction by not recording or by miscalculating votes.

Working in small groups, have students use Activity Page 55 to begin compiling information on candidates running for national, state, and local offices in their community. Among the offices students might choose from are the following:

NATIONAL   President, Vice President, Senator, Representatives

STATE   Governor, Lieutenant Governor, State Legislators

LOCAL   Mayor, City Council, Sheriff, County Commissioners, School Board

If students can find a picture of each candidate in the newspaper, a magazine, online, or in the candidate's campaign literature, this information can also be added. In the space marked "What We Know About the Candidate," the group might include the candidate's qualifications for office, a quote from the candidate that explains why he or she is running or expresses views on an issue. Collect the fact sheets in a special "For Your Information," or FYI, file. Set aside a special corner of the room for the FYI file. Put each fact sheet in a separate folder and add additional news clippings on the candidates as the campaign season progresses. After the election, have students record the outcome of the election on their fact sheet.

A good place to get a complete listing of local and state races is the county Election Board, the municipal or township clerk, clerk of court, or the voter registrar. Depending on the state, telephone numbers for these people can be found in the telephone book under such listings as Elections or Voter Registration. Another source for this information is the Federal Election Commission, 999 E Street NW, Washington, DC, 20463; 1-800-424-9530; http://www.fec.gov.

Electoral College

In the United States, the President is voted for twice. The first election takes place in November on Election Day when registered voters go to the polls to cast their vote for the person they want for President. This vote is called the popular vote. A second election occurs about one month after Election Day in December with a group of 538 people called electors. This group of electors make up the Electoral College. Their vote, not the popular vote, determines who will be President.

How It Works   On Election Day Americans are actually deciding how the electors will vote one month later. Explain to students that each state has a different number of electors. This number is based on a state's population. After each ten-year census (the last one was taken in 2000), the exact number of votes given to each state may be adjusted somewhat depending on whether the state has lost or gained population. In turn, the number of electoral votes each state has is equal to the total number of members it has in Congress: two senators plus the representatives in the House of Representatives. For example, California has 2 senators plus 53 members in the House of Representatives for a total of 55 electoral votes in the 2008 election. States with more people get more electoral votes than states with smaller populations, such as Delaware, which has

3 electoral votes. The District of Columbia has 3 electoral votes. In all, there are 538 electoral votes.

100	Senate
435	House of Representatives
3	District of Columbia
538	Total number of Electors

Normally, the electors for each state meet in their state capitals on the Monday following the second Wednesday in December. The electors cast their ballots, which are sealed and sent to the president of the U.S. Senate. The electoral votes are counted in a joint session of Congress, usually held in early January.

Who Wins? In each state, the candidate who wins the election for President gets all the electoral votes of that state even if the race is very close. In most elections, the candidate who wins the popular vote also has the largest number of electoral votes. For example, in 1996, Bill Clinton beat Bob Dole. Clinton received about 8 million more popular votes than the Republican challenger. He received 379 electoral votes and Dole picked up 159. In Arizona, Clinton won a close race with Dole, beating him by a little more than 31,000 votes. Yet Clinton received all 8 of Arizona's electoral votes. The official winner of the election for U.S. President is the candidate with the largest number of electoral votes.

A Bit of Election History

In the election of 1876, Samuel Tilden got almost 251,000 more popular votes than Rutherford B. Hayes. Yet Hayes had 185 electoral votes and Tilden had 184. The results of this election led to a bitter fight between candidates and their supporters. Each accused the other of cheating. The U.S. Congress appointed a 15-member electoral commission to determine the results of the election and the winner of the contested electoral votes. The commission consisted of 8 Republicans and 7 Democrats. Commission members voted along party lines. By just one vote, the commis-

sion gave the votes to Hayes. In March 1877, Hayes took the oath of office as the nation's 19th President.

The Hayes-Tilden election was the most fiercely contested election in the nation's history for more than a century. It stayed that way until the year 2000.

History Repeats In 2000, as in 1876, the candidate who won the popular vote did not win the election. Al Gore won the popular vote. He beat George W. Bush nationwide by about 500,000 votes. Bush, however, won the electoral vote in a bitterly contested election. This time, concerns focused on the election in the state of Florida. The election was a very close one and both candidates needed Florida's electoral votes to win the election.

On election night when the polls closed, George W. Bush had won the electoral votes of more states than Al Gore, but most of the states Gore won had large populations and, therefore, more electoral votes. For example, Bush won Alabama (9 electoral votes), Alaska (3), Arizona (8), Arkansas (6), Colorado (8), Georgia (13), and Kansas (6). In California, a majority of voters chose Al Gore for President. All 54 of California's electoral votes went to Gore. Winning just this one state gave Gore more electoral votes than the combined electoral votes of seven states whose citizens chose Bush for President. Gore won other states rich in electoral votes including New York (33), New Jersey (15), Pennsylvania (23), Massachusetts (12), Illinois (22), and Michigan (18). Bush won every state in the South. He also took many states in the West.

To win the presidency, a candidate needs 270 electoral votes. By the time the polls closed, Gore had 255 electoral votes. Bush had 246. Neither candidate had enough votes to be declared the winner. Both needed Florida's 25 votes to put them over the top. The election was too close to call on Election Day. Vote counting in Florida continued into the following day. When the machine count ended, election results showed that Bush had won Florida by fewer than 2,000 votes.

The Controversy In such a close election, Florida law required that the vote be recounted. At the same time voters in Florida's Palm Beach County filed a lawsuit challenging election results in their county. They argued that the design of the county's ballot confused many voters. They were especially upset by punchcard and butterfly ballot voting systems. They charged that some voters who intended to vote for Gore had mistakenly voted for another candidate. They also argued that new voting machines may have failed to count many ballots in which the holes were not completely punched through. In other Florida counties, voters challenged the results for other reasons. By November 10, a machine recount of votes in three Florida counties had shrunk Bush's lead. Fewer than 330 votes separated the two candidates.

Lawyers for the Democrats and Republicans asked the courts to step in and decide if the election and the recount had been fair. The Democrats wanted officials to recount the votes in some Florida counties by hand so that officials could determine whether ballots had been fully punched or properly marked. In a hand recount, a person looks closely at each ballot. No machines are used. Republicans opposed recounting the votes by hand. They wanted the recount stopped. They argued that it violated Florida election law. Lawyers took the battle over the recount to the Florida Supreme Court which ruled that recounts by hand were legal. The Florida Supreme Court ordered a hand count of nearly 60,000 ballots. Bush's supporters appealed this decision. By December 1, more than three weeks had passed since the election was held. Americans did not yet know who the new President would be.

The Outcome The U.S. Supreme Court agreed to review the decision of the Florida Supreme Court to allow a hand recount. It was the first time the Supreme Court had helped decide who would be President. On December 11, the justices heard arguments from lawyers for both candidates. Gore's lawyers argued that the statewide recount was legal. They referred to the 10th Amendment to the Constitution. This constitutional amendment gives states control over the election process. Bush's lawyers argued that the Florida Supreme Court had made new laws by allowing new deadlines for votes to be counted. A day later in a 5 to 4 decision, the justices agreed with Bush that the recount was illegal and stopped it, allowing Bush to add Florida's 25 electoral votes to his total. This gave Bush 271 electoral votes. Gore had 266. One elector from Washington, D.C., abstained. Bush won Florida by a margin of 537 votes out of the nearly 6 million cast in that state. Five weeks after Election Day the fight over Florida ended. George W. Bush became the nation's 43rd President.

The Top Ten

For this activity, the class will need Journal Pages 26 and 27 containing the map of the United States showing how many electoral votes each state has. Have students study the map and name the states that they think are likely to be most important to each candidate's strategy for winning the election. Have them find the ten states with the most electoral votes. Ask students to think about some ways the candidates might show that these states are important to their campaigns. (Students may suggest frequent visits to the states, large campaign organizations in the states, or spending more money on campaign advertisements and mailings in the states.)

Winner Takes All

Use this activity to help students see the difference between the popular and the electoral vote. As a class pick a Candidate A and a Candidate B for President. These candidates do not have to be living people. For example, they could be Abraham Lincoln and Thomas Jefferson. Students may prefer to choose non-politicians, such as musicians, actors, scientists, or athletes. Try to pick two candidates who are somewhat equally popular with students so that the vote is not a landslide in either direction. Have students cast ballots in a one-person, one-vote election. This will be the class's popular vote. After ballots have been cast and collected, divide the class randomly into six groups representing six different states: California (55), Idaho (4), New York (31), Rhode Island (4), Texas (34), Montana (3). Make sure that there are an odd number of people in each group so that there are no ties in the voting. Assign each group the same number of electoral votes as the state it represents has in the 2008 election. Within their groups, have students vote a second time for the same candidates. Students should vote as they did in the popular election. Emphasize that this is a "winner-take-all" arrangement with all the votes of the group going to the candidate with the majority vote. Tally the electoral votes from each group. Compare the results of the popular election and the electoral vote and discuss how it is possible for the two methods of election to produce different results.

Registration and Voting

Many students have no idea how citizens register to vote. Most are surprised to learn the process is relatively simple. Explain to students that there are three requirements for voting in the United States. Voters must be at least 18 years old, citizens of the United States, and residents of the town or city in which they want to vote. In many states (the law varies from state to state) people who have been convicted of a serious crime lose their right to vote while incarcerated.

Much like getting a library card, new voters must register, or fill out a special registration form. On the form new voters write their name, address, and date of birth and also must show some proof of their age, usually a birth certificate. The exact place of registration varies from state to state. New voters can register at the town or city hall, or by mail with registration forms available at public libraries or online. They can also register when getting or renewing a driver's license. Registration prevents election fraud. By registering every voter, officials make sure that no person

votes more than once during an election. On Election Day, each voter's name is checked off a list of registered voters in a particular area.

A Registration Simulation

To simulate the registration process, select five students to serve as members of the class Board of Elections. Board members conduct a voter registration drive. In the election simulation activity described on pages 31 and 32, this same group can also locate polling places, prepare ballots, and oversee the mock election. At this time, however, their main roles will be to write a description of voter qualifications for students who would like to register. Qualifications might be as follows: Voters must be U.S. citizens, at the school for at least 30 days, and over a certain age depending on the age of students in the class. Have students present their requirements, discuss them, and post the registration requirements in the classroom. Give the Election Board a copy of Activity Page 56. Have the Election Board members duplicate enough copies so that everyone in the class can have one, but do not give out the forms.

Set aside a corner of the classroom with a table for registration and a specified time, such as 15 minutes each day for registration. Have Election Board members set up a schedule for

DID YOU KNOW?

In 1972, the first election after the voting age dropped to 18, just over 43 percent (43.4) of 18- to 24-year-olds cast ballots. Turnout for this age group in the 2000 presidential election was a dismal 28.7. Less than a third of all young Americans voted. In off-year elections when there is no presidential election to get voters to the polls, youth turnout is even lower. From a high of 17.9 percent in 1974, it sank to a low of 12.1 percent in 1998.

sitting at the registration table and registering classmates using the Voter Registration Form. For added impact, registrars can have students repeat aloud a Voter Declaration:

> I am a U.S. citizen. I have lived in _____ (city) and _____ (state) for 30 days before the election. I will be at least _____ years old by Election Day. I am not registered to vote anywhere else.

If students are planning to have an election simulation, you may specify that registration will close at least one week before the election so that registration forms can be checked. Explain that students who are not registered will not be able to vote. When the registration period is completed, have the Election Board alphabetize the forms and make a master list of all registered voters on legal-size paper.

Get Out the Vote Posters

Explain to students that in recent decades the number of voters—particularly in the age group 18 to 24—has been dropping. There are many reasons for low voter turnout, but many non-voters don't believe their one vote will make a difference. As a class, have students discuss the following question: If it was your job to get new, young voters to register to vote, how would you do it? Have students brainstorm suggestions. Then, working in groups, have students make posters that encourage young people to register or explain how registration is done. Others might create special Get Out the Vote posters targeted to senior citizens, parents of young children, or people who have just become citizens. Posters could also have a theme such as Why Vote?, It's Your Right, or Voting Is Easy. Give an award for the five best posters and display them in halls or the cafeteria.

Some students may be interested in finding out more about organizations working to get out the youth vote. One such group is Rock the Vote.

DID YOU KNOW?

What concerns young voters? According to a recent poll, war, education, and the environment were key issues for young people. In interviews with young adults, many stated that the best way to increase voter participation is to have candidates talk about the issues that young people care about and draw connections between these issues and voting.

Rock the Vote
805 21st Street, 401
Washington, DC 20052
http://www.rockthevote.org

This organization was founded by the recording industry. It has street teams in 40 cities that go door to door urging young people to register to vote. They follow up voter registration drives with telephone calls, face-to-face canvassing, and pledge cards mailed back to people who have signed up to vote. The group makes commercials for youth-oriented radio and television stations such as MTV. They also appeal to young voters through their blog and other online resources.

Encourage students to discuss ways they can take action in an election even before they reach voting age. Among the activities they might identify are reminding adults to register and vote, becoming active in student council, passing out literature for a candidate, and keeping track of current elections. In many states elementary and middle school students are able to participate in mock elections that closely simulate actual presidential elections through an organization called Kids Voting. Look them up on the Internet (see page 5) to find out if Kids Voting has a program in your community.

Vote!

by Eileen Christelow
Clarion Books, 2003

About the Book

This nonfiction book is an easy-to read introduction to the election process for the lower grades. It is particularly interesting because it focuses on a local government election rather than a national one. This aspect of the electoral process is not often treated in books for young people. *Vote!* follows a town mayoral election from the beginning of the campaign to the final vote. It ends with a recount to mirror events of the 2000 presidential election. The book is narrated by two dogs who ask and answer kid-friendly questions about the election process. They explain why voting is important, and how political candidates work to attract voters. A timeline, glossary, and list of political parties are included at the end of the book. Vibrant cartoon drawings lend an accessible, comic-book feel.

While Reading

Vote! follows the election process from start to finish. As students read, have them create an election log, listing events from the mayoral race such as rallies, debates, polling, and the recount. Make sure students include at least five events. Next to each event, have students write one or two sentences about why the event is important. Have students share their answers in groups.

After Reading

Help students learn more about the election process by having them write a letter to an imaginary newspaper editor about either candidate Brown or Smith. The letter can explain why they support their chosen candidate, and students should focus on persuasive writing. They may also want to create a third mayoral candidate, and write a letter explaining why voters should support him or her instead of Brown or Smith.

Extension

Have students choose an issue that is important to their community. Work with the class to brainstorm a list of possible topics, such as new schools, better highways, year-round schools, air or water quality, placement of shopping malls, and more recycling or trash pick-up. Remind students that mayoral candidates often distribute flyers, put up posters, and send out mass mailings to citizens to show voters the changes that they want to make in their communities. Have each student create a poster for the issue that they have chosen. The poster should include a slogan and short statement that describes why the issue is important. Have students share their posters with the class.

Using the Media to Teach About Elections

During an election campaign, voters are bombarded with information about candidates. Research shows that many factors influence who the members of a political party choose as their candidate for President. Reports about candidates appear on television, radio, and the Internet, and in newspapers and magazines, public opinion polls, and advertising. All influence the way the public sees a candidate in the months leading up to the primaries and nominating conventions. Some of this information is objective—such as newspaper reports and analysis, television newscasts, and panel discussions by political reporters. But much of the information comes from the candidates themselves or from their supporters and is often biased. In television and radio commercials, Web sites, campaign literature, and speeches, candidates try to put themselves in the best possible light. Candidates want to get elected and their campaign materials are intended to convince readers and viewers to vote for them—and not for their opponent.

Looking carefully and critically at the media is an important skill that students can use throughout their lives. The activities that follow encourage students to analyze the media and to draw their own conclusions about the completeness and accuracy of election coverage.

Getting Started Begin this section by inviting students to suggest the many different sources from which voters learn about candidates: newspapers, radio and television newscasts and advertisements, the Internet, debates, direct mail

campaign literature, public meetings, and so on. List responses on the board. Discuss with students the kinds of information each source provides.

Critical Thinking

➤ *Which sources are likely to be most slanted or biased in favor of the candidate?*

➤ *Which sources are most likely to give an objective or unbiased picture of the candidate?*

Analyzing Print Media: Newspapers, Magazines, and Direct Mail

These activities will serve to familiarize students with the election information presented in newspapers, magazines, and direct mail. Students will also explore the difference between fact and opinion using editorials.

Election News Scavenger Hunt

You will need to collect newspapers published during a primary season or an election campaign in order for this activity to work. You might also ask each student to bring in a newspaper on a day when there is likely to be election news, such as the morning after a heated primary, a presidential debate, or a visit by candidates to the local area.

Before beginning, have students identify the various sections of the paper. Ask students which sections are most likely to contain campaign and election news (national and local news sections, editorial pages). Then divide students into pairs or small groups. Supply each group with a newspaper and Activity Page 57. Give students 15 or 20 minutes to complete their search. If students cannot find one of the scavenger hunt items in their own newspaper, you might have them trade newspapers with another group after a certain period of time.

Classes can also be divided into groups with local newspapers, groups with newspapers from the state capital or a different part of the state, or groups with national newspapers such as *USA Today*. Each group can make up its own Election News Scavenger Hunt, using the newspaper it has been given to create a list of election-related information. Have groups exchange newspapers and complete the scavenger hunt they receive. After the hunt is over, the class can compare and contrast the different types of information found in the different newspapers.

As a variation on this activity, give some groups magazines such as *Time* or *Newsweek* instead of newspapers. Students can compare the types of election information each offers.

Election Scrapbook

For this project, each student chooses a political candidate and creates a scrapbook about him or her. The cover can be made from a collage of campaign photos, brochures, and even bumper stickers of the candidate. Students should collect newspaper articles about the candidate and paste them on the interior pages. Students might also want to include quotations from the candidate, pictures of the candidate with the student's own captions, a short biography of the candidate listing his or her experience and qualifications, and a page describing the office for which the candidate is running. If students can find any political cartoons about the candidate, these can be included as well.

Analyzing an Election News Article

Have students bring to class news articles about candidates and election campaigns. Ask them to write a short summary of their articles and answer the following questions through discussion or in writing:

Critical Thinking

➤ *Does the headline seem for or against the candidate, or neutral?*

➤ *What can you learn about the candidate's stands on issues from this article?*

➤ *What can you learn about the candidate's qualifications for office?*

➤ *Are there any words or phrases in the article that suggest how the reporter feels about this event or about the candidate?*

➤ *Does the reporter use any words or phrases that influence your opinion or impression of the candidate?*

➤ *What impression of the candidate do you get from reading this article?*

➤ *What were some questions about the candidate that this article did not answer?*

➤ *Would this article help you decide whether or not to vote for this candidate? Why or why not?*

Comparing Headlines

In the summer of 1999 when George W. Bush was competing with John McCain, Steve Forbes, and other candidates for the Republican nomination, newspapers reported the results of a poll of New Hampshire voters which asked what Republican they favored for President. George W. Bush was already a strong favorite of many Republican voters. In this poll as well he was the favorite, getting the nod from 40 percent of those polled. John McCain was a distant second as the choice of 16 percent of voters. Headlines in three different newspapers reported the same results as "Bush Slipping with New Hampshire Voters," "Bush Holds onto Strong Lead," and "McCain Edges Closer to Bush."

Write these headlines on the board. Discuss the impression each adds to the poll results. Ask students to consider which headline puts a positive "spin" on the election results for Bush or for McCain.

Headline Collage

Divide students into groups. Assign each group a political candidate running in a current race. Candidates can be from national, state, or local elections, but should be candidates likely to be mentioned in local or state newspapers. Over a two-week period, have each group cut out or write down any headlines they see about their assigned candidate. If students have been assigned an incumbent, remind them that they can also look for articles about this official doing his or her job. At the end of the collection period, each group can make a drawing or collage of their headlines. Group members can pick out headlines that help or flatter the candidate and shade them one color and shade negative headlines with a different color. Students might also want to include a photograph of their candidate in the collage. The finished collages can be displayed on a bulletin board under the title "Election Headliners."

Write Your Own Headline

Look for articles about the outcome of an election, a candidate taking a stand or voting on an issue, or a campaign event attended by a candidate. Remove the headlines from the article. Give students copies of the same article. Have each student write a headline for the article. Compare headlines and notice how differences in wording influence impressions of the news report.

Help Wanted: Outstanding Leaders

Examine the classified section of the newspaper with students. Have students find examples of different kinds of job ads that list the education or skills required for the job. As a class, discuss the personality traits, skills, education, and experi-

ences that might help a person become an exceptional president, senator, governor, or mayor. Then have each student pick an elective office and write an ad describing their ideal candidate. Ads should include the skills needed for the job.

As a follow-up activity, post these ads on the bulletin board, grouping them by elective office, and national, state, or local level of government. As students learn about different candidates, have them pick one of the ads to answer. Have students write a letter telling why they think the candidate they have selected would be right for the job.

Speaking Up and Speaking Out

Discuss with students the differences between fact and opinion. Explain to students that the editorial page is a good place to read people's opinions on issues that are important to voters. Editorial pages often express how a newspaper's editors or publisher feel about issues of national or local interest. Point out the different types of features typically found on an editorial page: editorials by staff, syndicated columnists, local guest columnists, letters to the editor, political cartoons. As a class, name some of the key issues that concern people in your community now. Often these issues relate to schools, road construction, crime, affordable housing, government spending, public services such as police or sanitation, and environmental problems. Working in groups, have students use Activity Page 58 to analyze opinions on the editorial page.

Making Your Voice Heard: Letters to the Editor

After reading and analyzing the editorial page, have students select and describe one of the letters to the editor and write a response to it using Activity Page 59. Prior to assigning this activity, post on the bulletin board copies of five or six letters that students may wish to respond to. Before having students work on their own, consider picking one letter and discussing with the class the elements that might go into their responses. In responding, encourage students to follow these guidelines:

1. State the problem as the writer has explained it.
2. Explain why you agree or disagree with the writer's description of the problem.
3. Explain why you agree or disagree with the writer's solution to the problem.
4. Describe how you would solve the problem.

Politics in Your Mailbox

As the race to the election heats up, voters often receive campaign literature in the mail. Direct mail—or mass mailings sent to selected voters asking for support—is a form of campaign advertising. This type of campaign advertising usually has two purposes: to ask for money for the candidate and to gain votes. Often these letters are written by professional fundraisers hired by the candidate. Members of different groups may receive different versions of the same letter. For example, a person running for the state legislature might send one letter to members of a teachers' organization and a different letter to members of a veterans' organization. Ask each student to bring in an example of direct-mail campaign literature. Have students analyze the letters by considering the following questions:

➤ *Who wrote the letter? What is this person's connection to the candidate? Underline two or three sentences that tell why this person is writing to you.*

➤ *What does the letter writer want you to do?*

➤ *Can you learn anything from this letter about the candidate's position on campaign issues? about the candidate's qualifications for office?*

➤ *Does the campaign literature mention the candidate's opponent? If so, are any of the criticisms or charges against the opponent backed up with facts?*

Analyzing Electronic Media: Television

For many voters today, television is the major source of information about candidates for public office. Candidates come into our homes through our television sets in many different forms: commercials, newscasts, debates, talk shows, and panel discussions. Discuss the differences among these types of election coverage.

➤ *Which are likely to be the most objective? the most biased?*

➤ *Which tell the viewer only what the candidate wants us to hear?*

➤ *Do some types of television coverage give a clearer idea than others of a candidate's views on issues?*

Creating a Media Log

Have each student pick a candidate who is likely to receive a lot of coverage on local and/or national news. Distribute copies of Activity Page 60. Have students watch the nightly news for five days and fill in the log each time their candidate is mentioned. After students have completed their media logs, you might want to use these questions to generate discussion.

➤ *What can you learn about a candidate from watching television news? Can you learn about his or her views on issues? qualifications for the office? personal life?*

➤ *Can you learn enough from television news to make an informed decision about voting for that candidate?*

➤ *Did some candidates use the media more effectively than others? Give examples.*

➤ *What are some other ways to learn about local candidates? about the candidates for President?*

Comparing Television News

Divide students into several teams. Ask each group to watch the nightly news on one of the major networks or cable news channels for three days, using Activity Page 61 to record coverage of election news. One student in each group can be the timekeeper, keeping track of the amount of time the news show devotes to election news. Other group members can write two or three sentences describing the content of the reports. At the end of the three days, have groups prepare a group report based on their logs. Use them to compare and contrast nightly news coverage of the election on the different networks and cable news channels. Ask students:

➤ *Which network or cable news channel gave the most time to election news during this period?*

➤ *Did any give in-depth reports or analyses on candidate's views or experience?*

➤ *Were some candidates covered more often than others? If so, which ones? Why do you think this happened?*

Critical Thinking

Be Ad Smart

If possible, record and bring to class four or five examples of political campaign advertising. Be prepared to show each ad several times. Show students examples of both positive and negative political advertisements. Explain to students that in a positive political ad the candidate, his or her party, and/or the issues he or she supports are shown in a favorable light. The ad stresses the candidate, his or her family attachment, career achievements, and position on issues. A negative political ad portrays the opposing candidate in an unfavorable light. A goal of negative advertising is to make voters doubt the opposing candidate, his or her political party, or policies and the wisdom of his or her position on issues. Point out to students any examples of negative campaigning in the ads.

Another important factor to have students consider when analyzing a political ad focuses on who has actually sponsored the ad. Sometimes ads may seem to come from one of the political parties but in fact are sponsored by interest groups whose members and corporations will benefit from a win by the candidate they are supporting. Some of these groups are referred to as "527" groups, a name based on a related section of the Internal Revenue Service's tax code.

Have each student pick one advertisement and analyze it, using the questions on Activity Page 62.

The Art of Propaganda: You Can't Fool Me!

Candidates naturally want the strongest, most effective advertising they can buy. However, political advertisements often use propaganda, which is information that promotes a certain set of beliefs and opinions. In propaganda, opinions are often presented as facts. Usually propaganda is one-sided and does not tell the whole story. Listed below are some of the most common forms of propaganda.

Name Calling	Giving an idea or opponent a bad name.
Plain Folks	Showing viewers that the candidate is "one of us," just an ordinary person.
Card Stacking	Using facts and figures that favor one position while leaving out the facts and figures that support the other side.
Bandwagon	Trying to convince us to vote for a candidate because he or she is the most popular.
Testimonial	Having some well-known person voice their support for a candidate.
Empty Phrases	Using broad statements which mean little but create positive feelings, such as "I believe in freedom, peace, and the American way."

Have students view one of the recorded campaign advertisements introduced in the previous section. Using Activity Page 63, help students pick out examples of the different propaganda techniques listed above. Students can also keep track of various campaign advertising on Journal Pages 22 and 23.

Don't get bit by a sound bite. Ever since radio and television became important to political campaigns, candidates' messages have been getting shorter and shorter. A televised candidate speech that once lasted 30 minutes shrank first to a five-minute spot and then to the less-than-60-second message called a sound bite. In an effort to get their views onto the evening news, candidates often use sound bites that last 10 seconds or less. Discuss with students why sound bites might not be the best way to learn about candidates.

Lights, Camera, Action

Working in groups, have students use Activity Page 64 to create a storyboard for a 60-second television commercial for a well-known historical figure such as George Washington, Abraham Lincoln, or Thomas Jefferson. Each group will need multiple copies of the storyboard for this activity. Before beginning, have students identify the office the candidate is running for, the audience they would like to reach with their message, and what they want voters to know about their candidate. Encourage students to make up slogans for their candidate and include in their ads some of the candidate's views and qualifications. Using their storyboards as a guide, have students act out their commercials for the class. After each group has presented its ad to the class, students might use Activity Page 62 to evaluate one another's ads.

The Incumbent Advantage

As discussed on page 9, in many political races there is an incumbent and a challenger. Have students suggest reasons why, typically, the incumbent has a slight advantage over the challenger. For example, during the campaign period, the incumbents running for reelection make public appearances as part of their job. The activities of an incumbent President, member of Congress,

governor, and other high official often make the news, giving these candidates free air time on radio and television. Television viewers may see an incumbent President in a positive light while carrying out the duties of the office—making announcements from the White House, giving federal grants to states, visiting disaster victims.

Incumbents have another political advantage. They find it easier than their opponents to raise money for their campaigns. Because incumbents have won at least one election, they have become more knowledgeable about the political system. Usually they also have become more experienced fundraisers. Many big contributors to political campaigns prefer incumbents with established voter records, because their positions on issues are predictable based on how they have voted in the past. In addition, as members of Congress or other elective offices, incumbents already have some influence and experience. This makes them more attractive to potential donors than a candidate who is just entering the political process.

Students can see for themselves the incumbent advantage by tracking the appearances of an incumbent and challenger on nightly news for one week. Students can divide a sheet of paper in half lengthwise, label one side *Incumbent* and the other *Challenger* and make a mark each time the incumbent's name is mentioned and each time the challenger's name is mentioned. At the end of the week, have students add up the marks in each column and compare the results.

Analyzing Electronic Media: Internet

Over the last several elections, the Internet has become an increasingly helpful tool for learning about candidates and for getting out the vote. In recent years citizens have also started using the Internet to make government leaders and politicians aware of their opinions about the decisions these leaders make and to lobby for passage of bills they consider important. The Internet offers a variety of Web sites that help Americans find the names and e-mail addresses of the people who represent them in Congress and in state and local government. These Web sites make it easy for ordinary citizens to communicate directly with their representatives in Congress, expressing their views on political issues, legislation working its way through Congress, and other concerns. The White House receives thousands of e-mails daily from citizens who want to let the President know what they think of the job the nation's top leader is doing.

An Important Resource

The Internet has also become an important resource for candidates looking for volunteers to work on their campaigns and for potential donors. All major presidential candidates have Web sites where they can educate voters about their positions on issues and their political experience and raise money for their campaigns. Advocacy groups also help raise millions of dollars for various candidates. During the months leading up to a national election, many voters regularly receive e-mails from candidates and political parties urging them to visit a candidate's Web site or attend a rally or fundraiser for the candidate taking place in their community. For example, leading up to the 2004 election, Democratic presidential hopeful Howard Dean, former governor of Vermont, used the Internet to build a strong grassroots organization. A candidate little known as the race began, he built a following in cyberspace. According to George Washington University's Institute for Politics, Democracy & the Internet, by June 2003, Dean's supporters had created over 40 volunteer Web sites and spawned almost 300 online discussion groups. Through these online activities, Dean raised thousands of dollars for his campaign.

Some political analysts argue that a candidate needs one set of skills to be a successful political candidate on radio or television and a different set of skills to be a strong Internet vote-getter. Franklin Roosevelt mastered the art of getting his message across on the radio by projecting a sense of personal connection with his listeners. This sense of closeness or intimacy was especially evi-

dent in his fireside chats. Television is especially kind to people with good looks. In their television debates, the youthful and handsome John F. Kennedy proved to be a more popular television candidate than Richard Nixon. Television also favors candidates who can afford to spend large amounts of money on costly television commercials. Because third party candidates typically have less money and fewer staff members than candidates from the two major parties, the Internet helps get their message out to a wider audience.

Critical Thinking

➤ *Is the Internet making campaigning and elections more democratic? If so, how?*

➤ *What skills or attributes do candidates need to appeal people who follow a campaign on television? on the Internet? How are these skills similar and different?*

An Increasing Impact

Especially since the last presidential election in 2004, the Internet has had an increasing impact on campaigning. Candidates continue to use the Internet to generate interest and raise funds. It is a place where political hopefuls can engage citizens in spirited cyberspace discussions and gain supporters. It is a way to reach younger voters, appealing to those who spend a significant amount of time gathering information and socializing online. Aside from online discussion groups, candidates' supporters are also found on social-networking and video-sharing Web sites.

Just as television once brought the debates directly to the people in 1960, the 2008 election season has seen the advent of the "YouTube" debates. As a forum for average citizens to generate questions, people can post their questions to the Internet site via short digital videos. The videos are then played for the candidates, who must answer the questions in real time.

The Internet has helped open the lines of communication between those already in or running for political office and their constituencies. The sheer amount of information online can be overwhelming, however, especially for those who may find it challenging to distinguish fact from opinion. Discuss with students how to view information in election-related blogs, social-networking sites, and video-sharing sites with a critical eye.

Critical Thinking

➤ *How reliable is the information about candidates found on the Internet?*

➤ *Does information from the Internet have a greater or lesser influence on voters than that found on television or in newspapers?*

Key Web Sites

As listed on page 5, several Web sites provide timely and accurate information about candidates and the election process. Activity Page 65 gives students practice in using the Internet to gather information about candidates and elections. Before beginning you may want to review with students the basics of using their Internet browsers, such as typing in exact URLs and using hyperlinks. *Be sure to check the links yourself before using them in your classroom. This will insure that the material on the site is appropriate for your students. You will also be familiar with the content so that you can help students as needed.* Remind students that they don't have to read everything on the site. They can browse and skim until they find the information they need. Have them refer to the Activity Page regularly so they know what to look for next.

Answers to Activity Page 65
1. Marksense; 2. DRE Direct Recording Electronic; 3. paper ballot; 4. mechanical lever machines; 5. punchcard; 6. Thomas Jefferson, Andrew Jackson, Grover Cleveland, Richard Nixon; 7. John Kennedy, Jimmy Carter, George W. Bush; 8. Al Gore, Dan Quayle, William Mondale, Hubert Humphrey, Richard Nixon

Making Graphs and Taking Polls

In these activities students make graphs using election data they create themselves and analyze election data provided for them. They also take their own polls and think critically about public opinion polls reported in the press.

Graph It

Have students use Activity Page 66 to create bar graphs to analyze data. (You may want to enlarge the page to give students more room to fill in the graphs.) To begin, ask them to nominate "candidates" for a category such as best book, best television show, or best place to visit in the state. Once they've nominated several candidates, choose three that are popular with a wide range of students. Have students vote by a show of hands. Tally results on the chalkboard and then break down the results in three ways:

1. Total votes for each candidate.
2. Number of girls voting for each candidate.
3. Number of boys voting for each candidate.

Working individually or in small groups, have students make simple bar graphs reflecting the information shown on the board, listing the candidates in the same order on each graph they create. As each graph is completed, have the group write a sentence on a separate sheet of paper describing what they have learned about voters from graphing the information in each way. Students may find that some graphs give them more useful information about voting patterns than others.

What is your favorite sport?

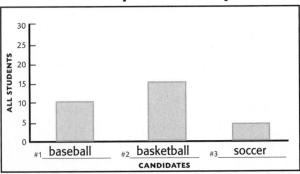

Using a Graph to Predict Voter Turnout

Students can use Activity Page 67 to make a line graph of voter turnout in presidential elections since 1968. For statistics on more recent elections, students can consult a current almanac. When the graph is completed, have students look for any trends in voter turnout. From 1968 to 1988, voter turnout generally declined. In 1992, the percentage of Americans who voted rose to its highest level since 1972. However in 1996, it dropped again to slightly less than in 1988.

In 2000 overall voter turnout rose slightly from the low in 1996, but it was still far lower than in 1960 when three-fifths of all Americans exercised their voting rights. Today only about half of all Americans go to the polls on Election Day. Among new voters, the age group 18 to 24, turnout is even lower. In the 2000 election, less than a third of all young Americans eligible to vote did so. Researchers say that young adults see voting as a choice not an obligation or civic duty. Polls show that many young people are torn between their civic duty and their belief that their vote doesn't count. Others say that volunteering at a soup kitchen, cleaning up a park, tutoring, or working with the homeless is a more important form of civic participation than voting. Discuss with students what they think might bring more young voters to the polls.

Polls and Pollsters

Explain to students that polls represent a "snapshot in time." Polls show how people feel about a topic at a certain moment, but do not necessarily indicate how people will feel about this same subject a week or a month later.

Give students practice in polling by having them take a school-wide poll. As a class decide on a topic and a set of choices for the survey. At lower grades, students might choose favorite animals. (*Which of these animals would you choose for school mascot: bear, leopard, cobra, alligator?*) For the upper grades, students might solicit opinions on local or national issues or issues that concern students at the school, such as the environment. (*Which of these issues concerns you the most?*) Or students can be polled on their choices for President. (*If the election for President were held today, would you vote for [candidate A] or [candidate B]?*) Ask students to poll 20 or 30 students at each grade level in the school. In recording responses, pollsters should be sure to record the gender and grade level of respondents. Some students can also be assigned to poll teachers. When the poll is completed, students can use Activity Page 66 to create a bar graph of their findings. Compare poll results for different groups polled such as boys, girls, teachers, or fifth graders.

Analyzing a Poll

Bring to class a political poll or survey from a newspaper or magazine. Also bring any articles that include conclusions that have been drawn from the poll results. As a class analyze the poll using these questions:

➤ *When was the poll taken?*

➤ *What questions were asked in the poll?*

➤ *Who was asked?*

➤ *How were the people who were polled chosen?*

➤ *How large a group was polled?*

➤ *Was the poll affected by a key event such as a military crisis, a natural disaster, or political scandal?*

Critical Thinking

➤ *Do you think answers to this poll might change if these same questions are asked in a week? in a month?*

➤ *Who sponsored the poll?*

➤ *Were any of the questions slanted or biased?*

➤ *Did any of the questions lead or encourage the person polled to answer in a certain way?*

➤ *What conclusions did the pollster or reporter draw from the responses?*

Literature LINK

The Kid Who Ran for President

by Dan Gutman
Scholastic, 1996

About the Book

In this satire of the political process, wisecracking Judson Moon, age 12, decides to run for President. In the weeks that follow, Moon stumbles through all the steps in a national campaign. He selects his polar opposite for a running mate. June Syers is an older African-American woman confined to a wheelchair who hasn't voted in a presidential election since she voted for FDR. They get on the ballot in their home state, garner lots of publicity, collect millions in campaign contributions, and even help to pass an amendment to the Constitution that eliminates the age requirement for the presidency. And despite a skeleton in his closet from the fourth grade, Judson wins the election. Fortunately, reality sets in and he resigns before even taking office, asking voters, "Are you out of your minds?"

The Kid Who Ran for President is a presidential campaign turned upside down. Moon knows nothing about politics or the Constitution when his campaign starts, but he is a quick learner. Gutman's presentation of the media circus that surrounds a campaign is hilarious.

While Reading

Have students keep a list of the steps that Moon and his campaign manager follow to get him elected, comparing each step Judson takes to the steps in an active presidential campaign. For example, Moon receives money without working very hard for it. How much money do the current candidates have in their war chests? How do they collect it? Ask students: How does Gutman poke fun at the political process? At several points, Moon tries to sabotage his own campaign. Why do his attempts fail?

After Reading

It takes a Constitutional amendment to allow Judson Moon to run for President, because the Constitution says a President must be at least 35 years old. Ask: What are the other requirements to be President? Encourage students to read the Constitution or look in an encyclopedia to find out.

If students could interview the author of the book what would they ask him? Have them write three questions that they would like to ask about his book, politics in general, or even the current election.

Extension

Invite students to write a new conclusion to The Kid Who Ran for President in which Judson Moon does not resign from office. Before they begin writing, have them look at some recent newspaper articles about the current President's activities. Ask: What might Judson Moon have done in similar circumstances? What sort of mistakes might he make? Do you think he would be able to accomplish anything? How does Judson's presidency end?. Does he finish his term or is he forced to resign? If students want to see what the author thinks happened to Judson Moon next, they can read the sequel, The Kid Who Became President (Scholastic, 1999).

Election Fever

During an election year, political activity in the United States reaches a fever pitch. Much of the excitement revolves around the two main political parties, the Democratic Party and the Republican Party. Although independent candidates have long exerted some influence on American politics, we still basically have a two-party system. In the following activities, students will gain an understanding of the role that these parties play in campaigns and elections. Election fever reaches its height right before the one day in November when everything is decided—Election Day. Students will learn about what happens on this important day and have a chance to simulate an election of their own.

Understanding Political Parties

Although you won't find political parties mentioned in the Constitution, they are very much a part of the American political system. In his Farewell Address to Congress, President George Washington warned against the harmful effects of political parties, believing they would do little more than divide the country. The first political parties were formed in the 1790s when Alexander Hamilton and Thomas Jefferson competed for President. Hamilton and his followers became known as the Federalists, while Jefferson's supporters became the Democratic-Republicans or Anti-Federalists. By 1809, the Federalist Party had lost many of its supporters, but the Democratic-Republicans remained strong. By the 1820s the Democratic-Republicans were known simply as Democrats. They have remained one of the two major parties to this day. In 1854 opponents of slavery formed the Republican Party. This party was created to oppose the expansion of slavery into the western territories of the United States. Today the Republican Party is the nation's other major political party.

The major political parties play many important roles. They recruit candidates to run for office and help them to get elected. Political parties also help to get out the vote at election time. Another important role of political parties is to bring important issues to the public's attention. Candidates and party officials discuss these issues in pamphlets, press conferences, speeches, and television appearances, helping citizens form opinions about them.

Design a Party Symbol

Have students describe some of the symbols associated with different political parties and discuss the different ways these symbols are displayed (banners, buttons, bumper stickers, posters). Ask students:

Critical Thinking

➤ *Why are political symbols important to a political campaign?*

➤ *Are they as important today as they were in the years before television?*

Have students work in groups to create a symbol for a new political party. Before beginning, students might consider what the party stands for and how the symbol might reflect their views. Have students pick a name for their party. Students might choose an animal, flower, abstract design, or set of initials as their symbol. Remind students that the symbol should be simple, eye-

Cartoonist Thomas Nast introduced the elephant as the Republican Party symbol in an 1874 cartoon in Harper's Weekly. Andrew Jackson first used the donkey as a Democratic Party symbol after his opponents called him a "jackass" in the 1828 election. Some years later, after Nast used the symbol of the donkey for the Democratic Party in a cartoon, it became widely associated with the Democratic Party.

catching, and easy to remember. For a bulletin board display, students can make larger drawings of their symbols on circles of heavy poster paper or oak tag. Or you can collect and display the symbols as a political button collage.

It's Party Time

Every four years the Republican Party and the Democratic Party hold national conventions. The most important activity at this convention is to nominate candidates for President and Vice President. Delegates also adopt a national party platform and make rules for governing the party. The convention usually lasts four days and is held in the summer months, during July or August, before the fall election. Students can keep track of these conventions using Journal Pages 12–15.

Here is a brief overview of what happens each day:

Day One: Delegates listen to the keynote address by a well-known member of the party. This speech is intended to whip up enthusiasm for the party. The speech sets the themes and the tone of the convention. Listeners also get a preview of the ideas and issues that the presidential candidate will stress in the election campaign ahead.

Day Two: Delegates discuss and accept the report of the Rules Committee which sets rules for the convention. The party platform, a statement of party principles and goals, is presented and approved by the delegates. The platform is prepared in advance by the Platform Committee, which has worked for months before the convention to create a document that party members can agree upon.

Day Three: The party's candidate for President is nominated. Prominent or up-and-coming members of the party give the nominating speeches. These speeches are followed by seconding speeches. Then the clerk of the convention begins a roll call of the states. The chairperson of each state delegation announces into a microphone how many votes his or her state gives to each candidate. The roll call is in alphabetical order. Today the nominee is always chosen after one round of voting.

Day Four: Since the election of Franklin Roosevelt, the presidential nominee of the party has chosen the vice-presidential candidate. However, it is common practice for the convention delegates to show their approval by officially nominating the vice-presidential candidate. On the last night of the convention, the candidates for President and Vice President give their acceptance speeches. By tradition, the presidential nominee gives the final speech of the convention. This acceptance speech is considered a highlight of the convention.

Balancing the Ticket

When selecting a running mate, candidates for President often try to choose a vice-presidential candidate who will attract more and different voters. Often the presidential nominee looks for someone from a different part of the United States. They might also look for someone who is younger or older to appeal to different age groups or someone who is more or less liberal or conservative than they are. This process is called "balancing the ticket." Once the tickets are announced, students can complete Journal Pages 16–19. Then in a class discussion, students can decide for themselves how geography and other aspects were factors in choosing a running mate for President in the current election. To extend the activity, you might have students work in groups to research how the balancing of tickets was achieved in recent elections.

And They're Off

After the national conventions, the race for the presidency switches into high gear. Candidates give speeches and more speeches, and travel across the country to rallies, dinners, and meetings. Candidates for other offices also work hard to promote their candidacies once the national convention is over. Candidates work to get their messages out to voters and spend more money on television, radio, and print advertising. The activities which follow give students a chance to explore the campaign process.

Day by Day

Contact the local campaign office of a candidate running for state or local office. Ask for a copy of the candidate's schedule for one week. Share this list with the class, looking at the types of events the candidate participated in and how these activities might have helped the candidate with his or her campaign. Ask students:

Critical Thinking

➤ *In what ways do you think the campaign schedule of an incumbent would be different from that of a challenger?*

Invite students to work with partners to track the campaign schedule of a candidate in a local, state, or national race for a week, using information from radio, television, and newspapers. Have them report their findings to the rest of the class.

Money, Money, Money

One of the biggest changes in campaigning over the last 50 years has been the skyrocketing cost of elections. Today presidential candidates spend as much time, if not more, raising money to finance their campaigns as they do talking with voters about their positions on issues. Candidates spend millions of dollars on bumper stickers, T-shirts, campaign buttons, billboards, and radio ads, but the most costly purchase is television time. Many political experts blame television ads for the rising costs of elections. With every election, television has grown more important. To build a national audience, presidential candidates must appear on television. Television puts presidential hopefuls into the homes of tens of millions of people.

Candidates raise money for their campaigns in several ways. They spend their own money. They receive contributions from individuals and interest groups. Their own political parties also provide support. One result of the high costs of campaigning is that wealthy candidates or candidates that are skillful fundraisers have an advantage. Political analysts worry that this advantage often has little or nothing to do with a candidate's ability to be a good elected leader. They point out that contributors who give money to a particular candidate may also expect that candidate if elected to give their needs and concerns special attention. In a democracy, the public good should always come first.

➤ *When making decisions that might affect the businesses of a big contributor, do you think elected officials may find it hard to be fair and impartial and act in the public interest. In what ways?*

Critical Thinking

➤ *Should there be a limit to the amount of money spent during a campaign?*

➤ *If yes, what sorts of changes might the public notice during a campaign season?*

On the Road With the Candidates

Display a large map of the United States on the bulletin board. Divide the class into campaign teams and assign each team one of the presidential candidates. Each team will follow their candidate on the campaign trail for a specified period of time. If the election has third party candidates, they should be included as well. Give each team different color push pins. Have students watch television and read newspapers and magazines to trace the movements of candidates on the map. Connect pins with same-colored yarn to show each candidate's movement during the campaign. Remind students of what they have learned about the Electoral College system. You may want to look at the map on Journal Pages 26 and 27. Have students list the top ten states in Electoral College votes and note the number of times their candidate has visited these states during the campaign. Ask students:

Critical Thinking

➤ *Are there any states the candidates have not visited? If so, which ones?*

➤ *Which states were visited most?*

➤ *What might be reasons that these states were visited more than others?*

Analyzing Campaign Speeches

An important part of every candidate's campaign is making speeches. Many voters decide whom to vote for based on their analysis of the various speeches a candidate makes. To help students become thoughtful analysts, record a televised speech by a candidate running for local, state, or national office. C-Span is a good place to find speeches to use. Before showing the speech, distribute Activity Page 68, and discuss the qualities students will be looking for as they watch the speech.

Students can also use this Speech Scorecard while they watch the televised presidential debates that occur close to Election Day. This will help them when they summarize their analysis of the key topics and issues covered during the debate, along with recording their general thoughts, on Journal Pages 20 and 21.

Step by Step to Good Speech Making

So that students can better understand how a convincing speech is constructed and delivered, share with them the steps listed on Activity Page 69. In particular, you may want to share these steps before the campaign simulation (see page 31), when students will have a chance to make campaign speeches of their own.

Classroom Campaigns and Elections

These activities offer a learning-through-doing experience. As students help plan an election campaign, they will have a chance to practice many of the skills they have learned in earlier activities, such as conducting a poll, creating a party symbol, and making and analyzing political ads and speeches. In the election simulation, students become aware of the consequences of the campaign and participate in the primary act of citizenship—casting a ballot.

Campaign Simulation

In this activity, students simulate the process of an actual campaign. At the lower grades, students might begin their simulation by voting for a book to read, television show to watch, sport to play, pet to care for, place to vacation, or food to try. You might want to use the "candidates" that students selected for their poll project on pages 24 and 25. Once the candidates have been picked, have students decide on criteria for judging the candidates. For example, if the class decides to vote on favorite desserts, students might assess their choices in terms of taste, nutrition, calories, time to prepare, costs of preparation, visual appeal, and so on.

Working in teams students can campaign for their favorite desserts, using posters, campaign buttons, or bumper stickers. They can make short speeches in favor of their candidates. Several students can play the Election Board and register voters for the election following the directions outlined on pages 14 and 15.

On Election Day, set aside a corner of the room for voting with a large ballot box. Board of Election members can enter the name of each voter in an election poll book as each student comes to vote. Activity Page 70 contains a simple, "official" ballot that can be used for voting. After ballots have been counted and a winner declared, discuss with students how they made up their minds about which candidate to vote for.

Ask students:

➤ *What reasons did you have for your choices?*

➤ *Were you influenced by posters and other publicity? by campaign speeches?*

➤ *Did the candidate's ads say anything catchy you remembered?*

➤ *Was there any negative campaigning? How did it influence your vote?*

Election Simulation

In this election simulation, students take on the roles of various participants in a presidential election campaign.

Assign Roles

The role cards on Activity Pages 71 and 72 provide roles for the following:

✔ **Candidate:** Choose two students for these roles.

✔ **Campaign Manager:** Choose two students, one for each candidate.

✔ **Press Secretary:** Choose two students, one for each candidate.

✔ **Speech Writer:** Depending on the class size, each campaign could have two or more.

✔ **Media Consultant:** Choose two students, one for each campaign.

✔ **Treasurer:** Choose two students, one for each campaign.

✔ **Pollster:** Depending on class size, an "independent" polling organization used by both campaigns might consist of three or more pollsters.

✔ **Television Reporter:** Depending on class size, choose two or more reporters.

✔ **Board of Elections Member:** Choose three members.

✔ **Independent Voter:** All remaining students can act as voters, along with those who have taken other roles.

Distribute Funds

Once role cards are distributed, give each candidate a certain amount of money (see Activity Page 73 for currency). Each candidate can get $12,000 or to make the simulation more interesting and realistic, one candidate can get $10,000 and the other $14,000. Encourage candidates to spend all their money. There is no advantage to having money left over. You may want to point out to students that in a real campaign the financial resources of candidates are not equal. Have candidates give their money to their treasurers. Give each candidate, treasurer, and the members of the Election Board a copy of Activity Page 74, which contains their rules for spending campaign money and a price list for campaign activities. Post copies of these handouts on the classroom bulletin board.

Distribute Activity Cards

After students have moved into their assigned groups, distribute the appropriate Activity and Roll Cards. There should be two groups made up of candidates and campaign staff (Campaign Manager, Press Secretary, Speech Writer, Media Consultant, Treasurer) and one group each of reporters, pollsters, Election Board members, and voters. After all groups have read over their Activity Cards, work with the class to determine the schedule of events that will make up the simulation. As the Activity Cards on pages 75 to 77 indicate, key events and activities can include television news broadcasts, press conferences, speeches by the candidates, registration, and voting. How much time students spend on these and other suggested activities will depend on how much time you have set aside for the simulation.

There are several options and once the class has decided, you may want to make a timeline to keep the simulation moving and on track.

Some classes may enjoy making up their own identities for candidates, but if students are having trouble getting started, you can also suggest identities for candidates. For example, one candidate might be a former governor from Massachusetts or from the students' home state. The other might be a former mayor, or a member of the Senate from Illinois or New York. Or, candidates can be modeled after individuals running for Congress or for local or statewide offices.

Review

Be sure to review with Election Board members the registration process described on pages 14 and 15. As candidates prepare their speeches, you might also review the aspects of good speech-making on pages 30 and 69 with students. You will need to work with the television reporters to decide when, where, and how they will hold their news broadcasts and show political ads by candidates. If your class has access to a video camera or digital recorder, students can create ads and news shows and show them at a certain time each day of the simulation. Make sure that all students know that on Election Day everyone votes, including Election Board members and candidates.

Literature LINK

Girl Reporter Rocks Polls!

by Linda Ellerbee
Avon Books, 2001

About the Book

This fictional work examines many important issues from voting and elections to peer pressure and popularity—from a teenager's perspective. *Girl Reporter Rocks Polls!* is part of Linda Ellerbee's Get Real series. It follows Casey, a smart, outspoken, and energetic sixth grader and aspiring journalist, as she tries to get the scoop for her school paper during student elections. She interviews other students, many of whom believe that elections are nothing more than popularity contests. This book tackles school elections and deals with such thorny issues as metal detectors in schools, privacy, and school cliques. Engaging and humorous, this novel provides insight into the many reasons why people run for political office. It stresses the difference between voting for candidates because of their stands on important issues, and voting for candidates because they are popular or members of the in-crowd.

While Reading

Before reading, have students write down a few reasons why they think someone might run for student council president. As they read, ask them to make a list of all four candidates in the book. Under each name, have them list the reasons why the candidate is running for office. They should also include some important traits, or characteristics, of each candidate. When students are finished, ask: *Are there are any reasons for running for office that the four candidates share? Are there good and bad reasons to run for office?*

After Reading

One of the most important issues in the Trumbull election is the debate over school metal detectors. Explain to students that before candidates run for office, they create a platform. A platform is a list of goals or changes the candidate would like to make if elected. Have students imagine that they will be running for student council president. Working in groups, have them brainstorm a list of school issues or problems and possible solutions to these problems. Now have each student create a platform for their campaign. Remind students that the platform should present solutions to problems that are affecting the school. Have groups present their platforms to the class.

Extension

Through her investigative journalism, Casey helps to change the outcome of the election. Explain to students that investigative journalism can help to keep our system of government honest and fair. Divide students into groups. Have each group find one example of mainstream investigative journalism using the Internet, television news, or local newspapers. Students should create a skit or presentation that explains the issue or story they have chosen to the class. They should include the name of the show or article, where it comes from, and why it is an example of investigative journalism. Ask students to consider whether the article or show they have selected seems fair or biased.

Election Wrap-Up

In the days and weeks after the election ends, newspaper reporters, political consultants, and "Monday-morning quarterbacks" fill the airwaves, the Internet, and print media with election analysis. They assess the winners and the losers of the 2008 Election, and offer their opinions on how the election results will affect the nation's domestic and foreign policy. For example, did politicians who supported the war in Iraq or favored bigger tax cuts do well with voters? Did those who opposed such policies get more votes than those who voted for them?

Election Night: Tracking the Election

Explain that on Election Day, students can use the map on Journal Pages 26 and 27 to tally the electoral votes each candidate has won as this information is presented on television. Have students point out the sections of the country where election results would be reported first and ask them to explain why this happens. As students are tracking election results, encourage them to look for "coattails" effects and any sign of a "landslide" victory.

On the days following the election, have students conduct their own analysis of election results by using their colored-in maps. Draw a "Results" chart (like the one shown) on the board. Volunteers can count the number of electoral votes each candidate received by region. Then have them use newspapers to find out how many popular votes each candidate received in each region. Encourage students to use the chart to compare the electoral votes and popular votes for each region. Have them circle the winning

Results

	ELECTORAL VOTES	POPULAR VOTES
Northeast		
Republican Party		
Democratic Party		
Third Party		
Southeast		
Republican Party		
Democratic Party		
Third Party		
Midwest		
Republican Party		
Democratic Party		
Third Party		
Southwest		
Republican Party		
Democratic Party		
Third Party		
West		
Republican Party		
Democratic Party		
Third Party		

party for each region. Then ask:

Critical Thinking

➤ *Did either presidential candidate win the election in his or her own state?*

➤ *Were there any regions in which the popular vote was close?*

➤ *If so, students can consider how might have a slight change in the popular vote affected the final outcome of the election.*

Concluding Activity

Have students create their own 2008 Election Wrap-up television show. Using Activity Pages 78–80 students can conduct their own analysis of election results. Begin by dividing the class into six groups. Assign five of the groups different regions of the United States: Northeast, Southeast, Midwest, Southwest, West. Duplicate and distribute the appropriate activity sheets to each group. To help them structure the information-gathering process, these activity sheets indicate which states in the region held elections for governor and Senate in 2008. Remind students that members of the House of Representatives face reelection every two years. Using newspapers, magazines, and online resources, have each group gather and analyze election results for their region. Put the sixth group in charge of gathering information on your local and state elections.

You might ask students questions like these to help them analyze election results:

➤ *Who were the big winners or losers? Did any candidates win by large majorities or lose by large majorities? Which political party won more seats in this election in your region?*

➤ *Compare election results in races for the House of Representatives and the Senate with the vote for President in your region. Did voters choose other members of the winning candidate's party for seats in Congress or for governor?*

➤ *Did the winning presidential candidate have long coattails in your region or your state?*

Critical Thinking

➤ *Were there any upsets or surprises in the elections in your region? Were any candidates defeated who were expected to win? Did any candidates lose who were expected to win?*

➤ *Were there similarities in voting patterns among the states in your region?*

➤ *Compare and contrast the regions. In what ways were the election results in this region similar to or different from the results in other regions? In what ways were they similar to results in your state?*

Have each group present the results of its analysis in a five-minute television skit. Encourage students to use visuals such as graphs or their Election Night maps for their presentations. They might also create political cartoons highlighting the election results in their region. Ask two students to serve as the show's anchor. These students might end the show by summarizing the trends or outcome of the election in each region.

Wrapping Up the Journal

If possible, have students watch live footage of the inauguration on January 20, 2009. Using Journal Page 28, students can follow along as the new President and Vice President take the oath of office. Students can then summarize the highlights of Inauguration Day.

To put the finishing touches on their journals, students can imagine themselves running for President. They'll list any important issues they would want to include in their platform, calculate the year they are eligible to run for President, and draw their own presidential portrait.

 **Name** _____

Government Fact Sheet

I am gathering information about _____.

kind or branch of government

Describe the officials who make up this kind or branch of government.

_____

_____

_____

_____

_____

How are the members elected or appointed?

_____

_____

How long are the terms of office?

_____

_____

Where do they work?

_____

_____

_____

What are their responsibilities?

_____

_____

_____

_____

_____

Electionary Game Cards #1

Polling Place:
a place where votes are cast in an election

Election Day:
the Tuesday after the first Monday in November

Registration:
signing up to vote by filling in your name and other information about yourself on a special form

Political Party:
a group of people who share similar ideas about how to govern the nation and work together to gain power by electing its members to public office

Primary:
an election between members of the same party who seek to be selected as their party's candidate

Delegate:
a person who is chosen to act for others at a meeting

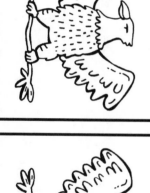

Candidate:
a person who runs for political office

National Convention:
a meeting of members of a political party to nominate a candidate to run for President

Electionary Game Cards #2

Electoral Votes:
the votes cast by members of the Electoral College. To win a presidential election, a candidate must win a majority of these votes.

Nominate:
to propose a candidate for political office

Inauguration:
the ceremony that includes the taking of an oath, which takes place at the beginning of a President's term of office

Opinion Poll:
a survey of people to find out what they think

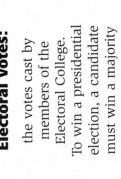

Incumbent:
a person already holding a political office

Sound Bite:
a fragment of television videotape, usually nine or ten seconds in length, especially broadcast during a news report

Landslide:
an overwhelming political victory

Third Party:
a party organized as an alternative to the two major parties

My **Election Journal**

Name _____

Glossary

candidate: a person who runs for political office

caucus: a meeting attended by members of a political party

delegate: a person who is chosen to act for others at a meeting or convention

democracy: a government of, by, and for the people, in which the people choose their leaders

Election Day: the Tuesday after the first Monday in November

electoral votes: the votes cast by members of the Electoral College (To win a presidential election, a candidate must win a majority of these votes.)

inauguration: the ceremony that includes the taking of an oath, which takes place at the beginning of a President's term of office

national convention: a meeting of members of a political party to nominate a candidate to run for President. (It usually takes place in the summer, a few months before the presidential election.)

nominate: to propose a candidate for political office

platform: a formal set of principles or goals held by a political party

political party: a group of people who share similar ideas about how to govern the nation and work together to gain power by electing its members to public office

primary: an election between members of the same party who seek to be selected as their party's candidate

third party: a party organized as an alternative to the two major parties

vote: a choice expressed by written ballot, voice, or a show of hands

voter: a person who votes

30

Contents

How to Use "My Election Journal"

This is your own Election Journal. You may use it to record the special events of the election season, information about the candidates, your thoughts about the election of the President of the United States, and more.

Feel free to paste pictures found in magazines or newspapers, draw your own pictures, or color the illustrations throughout the book. As you fill in the pages, you will be creating a wonderful record of this Presidential Election.

If I Were President . . .

If I were running for President in the 2008 election, these important issues would be part of my platform.

_____

_____

_____

_____

I am eligible to run for President in the _____ election.
election year

Draw a portrait of yourself as president.

President _____
your name

This is my journal about the

_____

Presidential Election

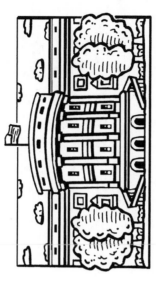

The President of the United States resides in the

_____ .

The address is

_____

_____

_____

Inauguration Day

On this day, the new President and Vice President take the oath of office.

Date of Inauguration is _____

The new President took this oath:

I do solemnly swear (or affirm) that I will faithfully execute the office of the President of the United States, and will to the best of my ability, preserve, protect and defend the Constitution of the United States.

Highlights of the Day

Candidates, Campaigns & Elections 4th Ed. © 2007 by Scher & Johnson, Scholastic Teaching Resources page 41

Qualifications for President

As stated in the United States Constitution, candidates for president must meet specific qualifications. Each candidate must be

✔ A natural-born _____ of the United States.

✔ At least _____ years old.

✔ A resident of the United States for at least _____ years.

On Election Day, every four years, voters pick a President and Vice President to lead the country.

This map has helped me track to the election. I have colored the states to indicate how each state voted.

Tip: Use blue for Democrat and red for Republican.

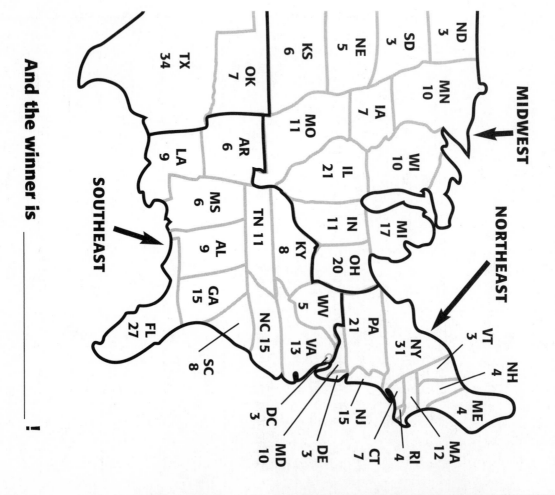

MIDWEST

NORTHEAST

SOUTHEAST

ND 3
SD 3
NE 5
KS 6
OK 7
TX 34
MN 10
IA 7
MO 11
AR 6
LA 9
WI 10
IL 21
IN 11
MS 6
AL 9
MI 17
KY 8
TN 11
GA 15
OH 20
WV 5
NC 15
SC 8
FL 27
PA 21
VA 13
NY 31
VT 3
NH 4
ME 4
MA 12
RI 4
CT 7
NJ 15
DE 3
MD 10
DC 3

And the winner is _____ !

Duties of the President

The head of the Executive Branch of our government is the President of the United States. The Executive Branch also includes the Vice President and the Presidential Cabinet. The presidential duties are as follows:

- to carry out federal laws • to recommend new laws
- to veto laws • to work with international powers
- to direct foreign policy • to command the Armed Forces
- to act as chief law enforcement officer
- to host ceremonial events

My Thoughts

_____

_____

_____

Ways to contact the President

Mail: The White House
       1600 Pennsylvania Ave NW
       Washington, DC 20500

Email: comments@whitehouse.gov

For more information, check out the Web site:
www.whitehouse.gov/kids/

3

How the Country Voted

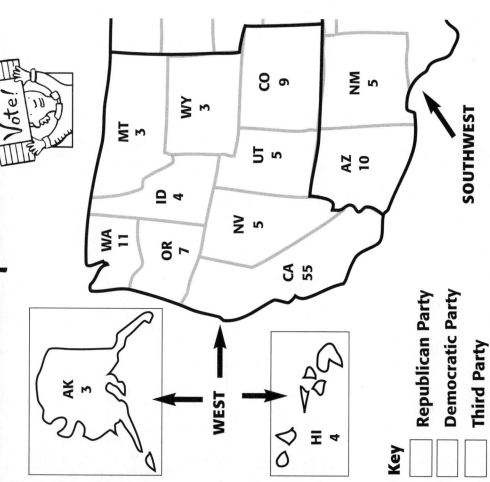

Vote!

WA 11
OR 7
CA 55
NV 5
ID 4
UT 5
MT 3
WY 3
CO 9
AZ 10
NM 5

SOUTHWEST

WEST

AK 3

HI 4

Key

☐ **Republican Party**
☐ **Democratic Party**
☐ **Third Party**

Totals:
Republican _____ Democratic _____ Third Party _____

26

Current Office Holders

The current President of the United States is

_____

President

_____ (photo oval)

Term of Office

_____ to _____

Age (when elected) _____

Home State _____

Political Party _____

Former Occupation _____

Family Members

_____

_____

Interesting Facts

_____

_____

4

My Thoughts

_____

_____

Highlights of the Day

_____

_____

4

25

The current Vice President of the United States is

_____

Term of Office _____

to _____

Age (when elected) _____

Home State _____

Political Party _____

Former Occupation _____

Vice President

Family Members _____
_____

Interesting Facts _____
_____
_____

Election Day

The National Presidential Election is held on the Tuesday after the first Monday in November every four years.

This year's election date was _____

Citizens of the United States voted for these winning candidates.

President _____

Vice President _____

Vice President

President

Candidates, Campaigns & Elections 4th Ed. © 2007 by Scher & Johnson, Scholastic Teaching Resources page 45

Political Party Symbols

THE DEMOCRATIC PARTY

The symbol for the Democratic Party is a _____.

THE REPUBLICAN PARTY

The symbol for the Republican Party is an _____.

6

Republicans

Bumper Sticker

TV Ads Say . . .

My Thoughts

_____

_____

_____

_____

_____

_____

_____

6   23

The Campaign Begins

The following people have announced their desire to be President.

Democratic Party

Republican Party

Other Party Candidates

Campaign Advertisements
Democrats

Bumper Sticker

TV Ads Say . . .

My Thoughts

Countdown to the Conventions

Most primaries and caucuses take place between January and June of a presidential election year. In these elections, voters decide who will be their state's nomination for each party. Delegates from each state then attend the National Conventions where each party's candidates are chosen.

Record the dates and winners of each state's primary election or caucus.

Date	State	Primary or Caucus	WINNERS		
			Democrat	Republican	Other Party
	Alabama				
	Alaska				
	Arizona				
	Arkansas				
	California				
	Colorado				
	Connecticut				
	Delaware				
	District of Columbia				
	Florida				
	Georgia				
	Hawaii				
	Idaho				

☆ ☆ ☆ ☆

Vice-Presidential Debates

☆ ☆ ☆

☆ ☆ ☆

Dates _____

Topics and Issues

_____

_____

_____

_____

My Thoughts

_____

_____

_____

_____

_____

_____

Date	State	Primary or Caucus	WINNERS		
			Democrat	Republican	Other Party
	Illinois				
	Indiana				
	Iowa				
	Kansas				
	Kentucky				
	Louisiana				
	Maine				
	Maryland				
	Massachusetts				
	Michigan				
	Minnesota				
	Mississippi				
	Missouri				
	Montana				
	Nebraska				
	Nevada				
	New Hampshire				
	New Jersey				
	New Mexico				

★ VOTE ★

Debates

☆ ☆ ☆ ☆ ☆

Presidential Debates

☆ ☆ ☆ ☆

Dates _____

Topics and Issues

_____
_____
_____
_____

My Thoughts

_____
_____
_____
_____

Candidates, Campaigns & Elections 4th Ed. © 2007 by Scher & Johnson, Scholastic Teaching Resources page 49

★VOTE★

Date	State	Primary or Caucus	WINNERS		
			Democrat	Republican	Other Party
	New York				
	North Carolina				
	North Dakota				
	Ohio				
	Oklahoma				
	Oregon				
	Pennsylvania				
	Rhode Island				
	South Carolina				
	South Dakota				
	Tennessee				
	Texas				
	Utah				
	Vermont				
	Virginia				
	Washington				
	West Virginia				
	Wisconsin				
	Wyoming				

Republican
Vice-Presidential
Candidate

Home State _____

Age _____

Former Occupation _____

Family Members _____

Interesting Facts _____

My Thoughts _____

Candidates, Campaigns & Elections 4th ed. © 2007 by Scher & Johnson Scholastic Teaching Resources page 50

My State's Results

My state is _____.

The date of our _____ is _____.
Primary/Caucus/Other

★ THE WINNERS! ★

Democrat _____

Republican _____

Third Party _____

Pictures of the Winners

Getting to Know the Candidates

Republican
Presidential
Candidate

Home State _____

Age _____

Former Occupation _____

Family Members _____

Interesting Facts _____

_____

_____

My Thoughts _____

_____

_____

Political Party Conventions

The Democratic Convention

☆ ☆ ☆ ☆
☆ ☆ ☆ ☆
☆ ☆ ☆ ☆

City _____

Dates _____

The delegates at the Democratic National Convention chose these candidates:

Presidential Candidate _____

Vice-Presidential Candidate _____

Pictures of the Candidates

12

Democratic
Vice-Presidential
Candidate

Home State _____

Age _____

Former Occupation _____

Family Members _____

Interesting Facts _____
_____

My Thoughts _____
_____
_____

The main topics and issues at the convention were

_____
_____
_____
_____
_____
_____
_____
_____
_____
_____

Getting to Know the Candidates

Democratic Presidential Candidate

Home State _____

Age _____

Former Occupation _____

Family Members _____

Interesting Facts _____
_____
_____

My Thoughts _____
_____
_____

Candidates, Campaigns & Elections 4th Ed. © 2007 by Scher & Johnson, Scholastic Teaching Resources, page 53

Political Party Conventions

☆ ☆ ☆ ☆ ☆ ☆
The Republican Convention
☆ ☆ ☆ ☆ ☆ ☆ ☆ ☆

City _____

Dates _____

The delegates at the Republican National Convention chose these candidates:

Presidential Candidate _____

Vice-Presidential Candidate _____

Pictures of the Candidates

The main topics and issues at the convention were

_____
_____
_____
_____
_____
_____
_____
_____
_____
_____

Candidates, Campaigns & Elections 4th Ed. © 2007 by Scher & Johnson, Scholastic Teaching Resources page 54

 **Name** _____

Election Fact Sheet

Office _____

Name of Candidate _____

Political Party _____

What We Know About the Candidate

_____

_____

_____

_____

_____

_____

_____

_____

_____

_____

_____

If available,
place picture of
candidate here.

_____

_____

_____

_____

_____

Outcome _____ Date _____

Prepared by _____

Voter Registration Form

Last Name _____

First Name _____

Address

(Number and Street) _____

_____

_____

City _____   County _____

State _____

Date of Birth _____

Place of Birth _____

Signature _____

Date _____

Witness _____

Date _____

City or town where registration was held

_____

Warning! If you sign this card and know it to be false, you can be convicted of a crime and jailed for up to five years, or fined, or both.

Candidates, Campaigns & Elections 4th Ed. © 2007 by Scher & Johnson, Scholastic Teaching Resources page 56

Name _____

Election News Scavenger Hunt

Find at least eight of the items on the list below in the newspaper you have been given, and check them off the list. Be sure to write down the page number on which you locate each item.

Name of Newspaper _____

Newspaper's Date _____

Item	Page Number
1. ❑ Photo of a candidate	_____
2. ❑ Headline about a candidate or election	_____
3. ❑ Quotation from a candidate	_____
4. ❑ Article about a candidate running for national office	_____
5. ❑ Article about a candidate running for state office	_____
6. ❑ Article about a candidate running for local office	_____
7. ❑ Names of two elected offices (for example, mayor or governor)	_____
8. ❑ Name of the Democratic Party candidate	_____
9. ❑ Name of the Republican Party candidate	_____
10. ❑ Letter to the editor about an election	_____
11. ❑ Editorial about an election	_____
12. ❑ A cartoon about campaigns or elections	_____

Your Opinion Please

1. Check any of the features listed below that you find on the editorial page you have been given.

   ❏ letters to the editor   ❏ editorials by newspaper staff members

   ❏ local guest columnists   ❏ comic strips

   ❏ syndicated columnists   ❏ political cartoons

   Describe any other features on the page not listed above. _____

   _____

2. Describe one issue that concerns the editors of the newspaper you are using.

   _____

   _____

   _____

3. What does the editorial writer think should be done about this issue?

   _____

   _____

   _____

4. Did you find any editorials or cartoons about local issues that directly affect or concern people in your community or state? Give one example of a local issue.

   _____

   _____

5. Did you find any editorials or cartoons about national issues that affect people throughout the United States? Give one example of a national issue.

   _____

   _____

6. List five words that the editorial writer uses that show that this is an opinion rather than fact.

   1. _____

   2. _____

   3. _____

   4. _____

   5. _____

Making Your Voice Heard

1. Describe one issue that concerns someone who has written a letter to the editor. Attach a copy of the letter to this activity sheet.

_____

_____

_____

_____

_____

2. Write your own letter in response to a letter to the editor that has appeared in the newspaper.

Dear _____ :

_____

_____

_____

_____

_____

_____

_____

_____

_____

_____

_____

_____

_____

3. Choose an issue in your community or school about which you feel strongly, such as a recycling program, a new playground, or a new building or highway. Write a letter to the editor of your local newspaper or school newspaper expressing your opinion on this issue.

Name _____

Media Log _____
type of media

Date	Summary of News Item	Helpful or Harmful to the Candidate?
		❏ Helpful ❏ Harmful
		❏ Helpful ❏ Harmful
		❏ Helpful ❏ Harmful
		❏ Helpful ❏ Harmful
		❏ Helpful ❏ Harmful

Name _____

Television News Election Log

Network or Cable Channel _____

Time of Broadcast _____

Name of Show_____

Date	Summary of News Item	Length of Item in Minutes	Candidates' Views
			❑ Yes ❑ No
			❑ Yes ❑ No
			❑ Yes ❑ No
			❑ Yes ❑ No
			❑ Yes ❑ No

Total time in minutes _____

Be Ad Smart

Use this page to study the secret meaning of a candidate's television advertisement and to find out the story behind the story. Write your answers on the back of this page or on another sheet of paper.

Name of Candidate _____

Position he or she is running for _____

1. Does the candidate appear in the ad? If so, what is he or she doing?

2. Do any other people appear in the ad with the candidate? If so, what is their part in the ad?

3. What did you learn about the candidate's stand on issues?

4. What did you learn about the candidate's qualifications for public office?

5. Did the candidate's organization sponsor the ad? If yes, did the ad try to influence your opinion of his or her opponent? If so, in what way?

6. If the candidate's organization did not sponsor the ad, who did?

7. Were music or sound effects important to the overall impression of the ad?

8. Was the setting important to the overall impression of the ad?

9. Does the ad use any special slogans to get the candidate's message across?

10. What group of people did the makers of this ad want to appeal to? For example, was this ad aimed at all voters, younger voters, women, senior citizens, or some other group?

11. What special images or props were used?

12. What impression did you have of the candidate after viewing this ad?

13. Do you think this is the impression the ad's sponsor wanted you to have? Explain.

The Art of Propaganda: You Can't Fool Me!

Propaganda comes in many different flavors. Use this page to examine a campaign advertisement and to keep track of the different types of propaganda the candidate uses.

Type of Propaganda	Example
Name Calling	
Plain Folks	
Card Stacking	
Bandwagon	
Testimonial	
Empty Phrases	

Lights, Camera, Action

Scene # _____
Script

_____

_____

_____

_____

_____

Visual

Scene # _____
Script

_____

_____

_____

_____

_____

Visual

Scene # _____
Script

_____

_____

_____

_____

_____

Visual

Internet Scavenger Hunt

Throughout the United States, the nation's cities and towns have many different kinds of voting systems. Items 1 to 5 each describe a different voting system. Fill in the blank with the name of one of the voting systems below.

DRE	Marksense	Paper Ballot	Mechanical Lever Machine	Punchcards

1. Voters mark their choices on a ballot card using a special kind of pen. Next to each candidate's name is an empty rectangle, circle, or arrow. Voters fill in the empty symbol with the special pen. After completing their ballots, they feed them into a computer that reads the votes electronically.

_____

2. This electronic machine does not have a paper ballot. Voters enter their choices on a touch screen. The machine has a keyboard that allows the voter to enter the names of write-in votes. The choices are electronically stored in the machine's memory and added automatically to the choices of all other voters.

_____

3. This type of ballot was first used in the United States in 1889. Voters record their choices by marking boxes next to a candidate's name. They drop their completed ballots into a sealed ballot box. Today less than 2 percent of all registered votes use this kind of voting system. It is mostly used in small towns and rural areas.

_____

4. Voters pull levers on a large voting machine to indicate their choices. However, factories no long make these kinds of voting machines. Election officials are replacing them with computer-operated systems.

_____

5. Voters use a special device to punch holes in a card next to the names of the candidates they choose. After voting, the voter feeds the ballot into a computer that automatically counts each vote. Many counties are now switching from this voting system to newer, more advanced electronic systems.

_____

6. Four Americans who tried a first time to win the presidency and failed went on to win one or more terms as President some years later. Who are they?

_____

_____

7. In the last 50 years only three candidates have been elected President without winning the state of California. Who are they?

_____

_____

8. For most candidates, serving as U.S. Vice President hasn't been a very good path to the presidency. Since 1960 five Vice Presidents have tried and failed to win the presidency. Some lost their party's nomination. Others lost the general election. Who are two former Vice Presidents that have run for President since 1960 and lost?

_____

_____

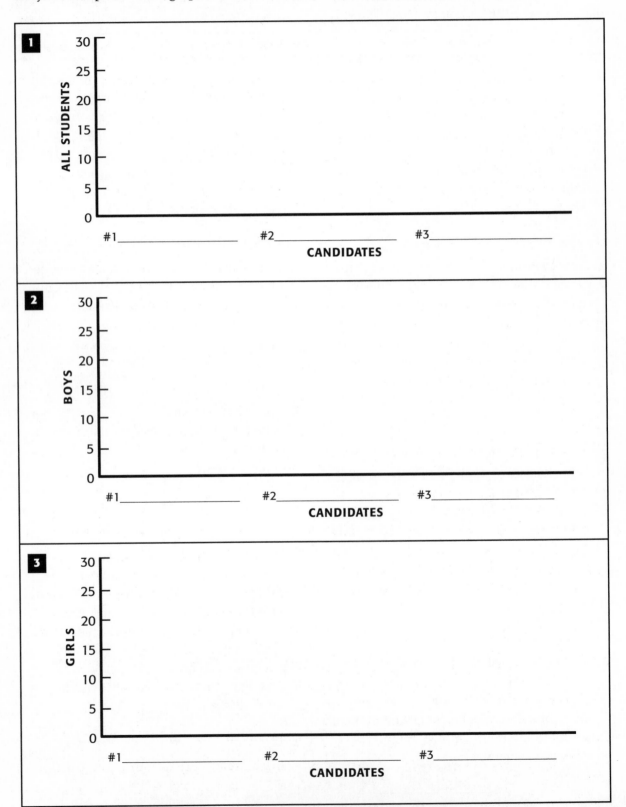

Graph It

Use the voting information your teacher has given you to complete these bar graphs. As you complete each graph, write a sentence about what you learned from it.

1

ALL STUDENTS

30
25
20
15
10
5
0

#1_____ #2_____ #3_____

CANDIDATES

2

BOYS

30
25
20
15
10
5
0

#1_____ #2_____ #3_____

CANDIDATES

3

GIRLS

30
25
20
15
10
5
0

#1_____ #2_____ #3_____

CANDIDATES

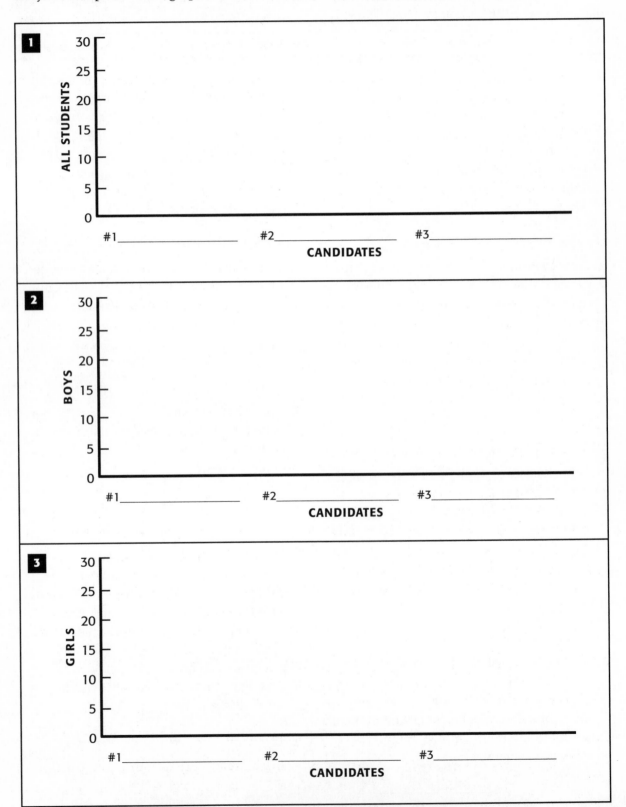

Name _____

Americans at the Polls

Use the information in the Data box to complete this graph. Include data about more recent elections by researching in an almanac or encyclopedia. Draw points for each of the years and then connect the points to form a line graph.

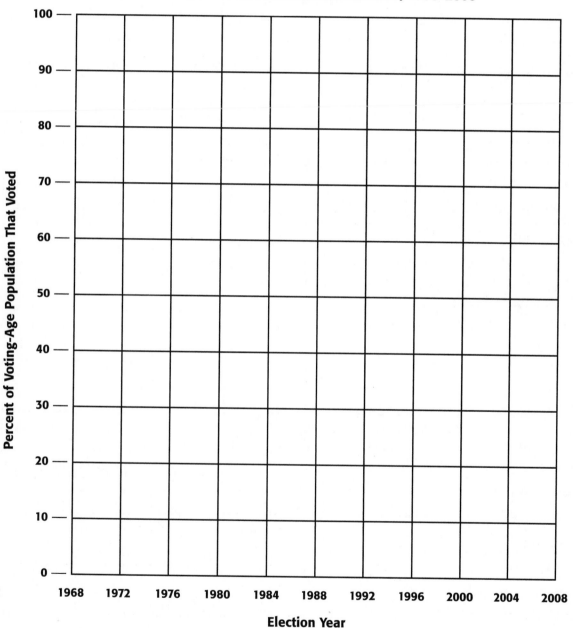

Voter Turnout in U.S. Presidential Elections, 1968–2008

Percent of Voting-Age Population That Voted

100 90 80 70 60 50 40 30 20 10 0

1968 1972 1976 1980 1984 1988 1992 1996 2000 2004 2008

Election Year

DATA										
1968	**1972**	**1976**	**1980**	**1984**	**1988**	**1992**	**1996**	**2000**	**2004**	**2008**
60.8	55.2	53.5	52.5	53.1	50.1	55.1	49.1	51.3	_____	_____

Speech Scorecard

Use this scorecard to analyze a candidate's speech and to grade the various parts of the speech.

Speaker's Name _____

Occasion for Speech _____

Date _____

	Excellent	Good	Fair	Poor
Opening of speech				
Awareness of audience				
Organization of speech				
Choice of language				
Forcefulness				
Sincerity				
Eye contact				
Preparedness				
Gestures				
Length of speech				

Based on this speech, I'd vote for the candidate: ❑ Yes ❑ No

Candidates, Campaigns & Elections 4th Ed. © 2007 by Scher & Johnson, Scholastic Teaching Resources page 68

Step by Step to Good Speech Making

Planning Your Speech

1. Be prepared. You may be a little nervous, but that may be a good thing. Your nervousness may help you put a little extra energy into your speech.

2. Consider your audience. What do you know about the group? What are their needs? Do they already agree with you? Or do you need to change their minds?

3. When you plan your speech, keep it simple. Use ordinary language and simple easy-to-follow sentences. Repeat your key points in different words.

4. Always begin with something to capture the attention of the audience—a joke, a story, an extraordinary statement, a challenge.

5. Stress what you want your audience to do—vote for you or vote for your candidate.

6. Timing is important. Don't speak too long; don't end too quickly.

7. End your speech with a summary of what you've said and a call to action—you want listeners to vote for you.

Practice, Practice, Practice

8. Practice saying your speech aloud. Ask your family and friends to listen to you and to offer suggestions. Record a rehearsal and then watch your performance.

9. Pay attention to your tone of voice and your gestures.

10. Do not read your speech. Use note cards or an outline. Speak directly to your audience as much as possible.

Delivering Your Speech

11. Look at your audience. Make eye contact.

12. Speak clearly. Don't speed up or go too fast.

13. Don't pace, scratch, or push your hair back. All gestures should have a purpose.

Official Ballot of _____

Office _____

    ❑ Candidate 1 _____

    ❑ Candidate 2 _____

    ❑ Candidate 3 _____

    ❑ Candidate 4 _____

Official Ballot of _____

Office _____

    ❑ Candidate 1 _____

    ❑ Candidate 2 _____

    ❑ Candidate 3 _____

    ❑ Candidate 4 _____

Official Ballot of _____

Office _____

    ❑ Candidate 1 _____

    ❑ Candidate 2 _____

    ❑ Candidate 3 _____

    ❑ Candidate 4 _____

Election Simulation Role Cards

Candidate

You are running for the office of President of the United States. Your job is to campaign for office by making speeches, appearing in television campaign ads and at press conferences, and talking with voters about your goals and plans. You will need to work closely with your campaign manager to supervise the work of your campaign staff.

Campaign Manager

Your job is to supervise the work of your campaign staff. This group consists of a press secretary, speech writer, and media consultant. You can hire a polling organization to help you decide how well the campaign is going or to decide what issues voters care about. You will work closely with the candidate and the members of your staff to plan a campaign that makes your candidate and his or her ideas well known. You will also work closely with the treasurer to decide how campaign advertising funds should be spent. Another part of your job is to recruit campaign workers from among voters to distribute flyers, put up posters, or take part in rallies.

Press Secretary

You will work with the campaign manager and media specialist to send out press releases about your candidate to the television reporters. You can hold a press conference and invite newspaper and television reporters to attend.

Speech Writer

Your job is to write election speeches for your candidate, telling why you think he or she should be elected. You can also create campaign posters, flyers, and brochures about your candidate and work with the media consultant on television ads.

Media Consultant

You are a media specialist. Your job is to plan your candidate's television commercials and any other advertising. You will be working hard to create a good image for your candidate. You will advise the candidate on what campaign appearances to make, how to dress for public appearances, and what to say. You can create political ads for your candidate and hire actors from the pool of independent voters to appear in your commercials. You will also work closely with the speech writers to prepare posters and any other campaign literature.

Election Simulation Role Cards

Treasurer

$ Your job is to work with the candidate and the campaign staff to decide how the campaign advertising money will be spent. You must hold onto and keep track of the money given to your candidate, give it out when requested to do so by the candidate or campaign manager, and let the candidate know often how much money has been spent. Your teacher will tell you how much money your campaign has to spend.

Pollster

You belong to a company that conducts polls for political candidates. Your job is to find out what issues concern voters and report your findings to the candidates that hire you. You also take polls in which you question voters about their impressions of the candidate and find out how much support a candidate has. This information helps candidates plan their campaigns. Such information helps them make key decisions about how much money to spend on advertising and how this money can be spent wisely.

Television Reporter

Your job is to report on the campaign to the television audience on your daily news broadcast. You can interview the candidates at press conferences, analyze campaign ads, and report on speeches given by the candidates. You can also report the results of polls taken by pollsters.

Election Board Member

Your job is to supervise the election. You will need to find a polling place for students to vote on Election Day, make sure ballots are printed, and direct the elections so that all students who have registered have a chance to vote. You will create a poll book, give out ballots, open and close the polls, count the ballots, and announce the winner of the election.

Independent Voter

[X] Your job is to listen to the campaign speeches of the candidates, participate in polls when asked, take part in campaign rallies or hand out leaflets for the candidate of your choice, register to vote, think carefully about which candidate would make the best president, and vote on election day.

Campaign Funds

Copy this page eight times, cut out bills as indicated for a total of $24,000. Use as currency for the Election Simulation.

The Rules for Spending Campaign Money

1. Campaign money can only be spent on these five items: television political ads, polls, campaign brochures, posters, and flyers.

2. Every time you make and show a political ad on television, you must pay the Election Board.

3. Every time you make and give out a new campaign brochure or flyer, you must pay the Election Board.

4. Every time you put up a poster, you must pay the Election Board.

5. Every time you have a new poll taken, you must pay the Election Board.

6. When you have spent your campaign money, you will not get any more and you cannot borrow money from anyone else.

Price List for Campaign Activities	
Show a campaign ad on television	$2,500
Give out campaign brochure to voters	$1,000
Give out flyers to voters	$500
Conduct a poll	$1,500
Put up a poster	$500

Candidate and Campaign Staff

1. Pick a party name and symbol.

2. Identify issues that the candidates and campaign staffs consider important and appealing to voters. These can be national issues, local issues, or schoolwide issues.

3. Decide on a budget for the campaign and make a list of ways for the candidate to get his or her ideas known to voters and the media.

4. Issue a press release to the media and/or flyers to voters announcing candidacy.

5. Contact polling organization or pollsters to conduct a poll to find out how voters feel about issues candidates have chosen to run on.

6. Hold a press conference or record a political ad for television.

7. Make posters and flyers.

8. Recruit campaign workers to put up posters and give out campaign literature.

9. Hold a campaign rally.

10. Prepare a speech to be given before the election.

11. Hold a press conference to react to something the opposing candidate has said or done.

12. Challenge the opposing candidate to a debate.

13. Seek endorsements from members of the class and put them in campaign literature or post them on the bulletin board.

14. Hold another press conference or record another political ad for television.

15. Try to get some free air time on television by staging a "photo opportunity" like a visit with voters.

16. Give an election speech at a rally or on television.

17. Election Day: Make sure campaign staff and campaign workers get out the vote.

Board of Election Members

1. If voters have not registered, ask your teacher to make copies of the Voter Registration Form. Begin a voter registration drive. Put a sign on the bulletin board announcing the deadline for registering. Try to get all class members to register. Explain that only people who have registered will be allowed to vote.

2. After the deadline for registration has passed, collect and alphabetize registration forms and create a Poll Book of all registered voters.

3. Find and set up a polling place for Election Day.

4. Fill in the names of candidates and their political party on an Official Ballot and make enough copies of the ballot for everyone in the class to vote.

5. Make a ballot box.

6. Post a copy of The Rules for Spending Campaign Money on the bulletin board and find out from the teacher how much money each candidate was given.

7. Decide how you will make sure that the rules for spending campaign money are being followed by all candidates.

8. Decide on penalties for spending money improperly and report these decisions to the television reporters, candidates, campaign staff, and voters.

9. Keep a list of how much money each candidate has spent and let candidates know when they have spent all of their money.

10. On Election Day open the polls and show the class that the ballot box is empty.

11. Before voters get their ballots, make sure their names are in the Poll Book. Be sure to mark off their names after giving them their ballots.

12. After everyone has voted announce that the polls are closed and count the ballots.

13. Announce election results.

Pollsters

1. Make up a name for your polling organization.

2. Let candidates and news reporters know that you are a polling organization and will conduct polls for them. You may want to make an announcement on television or make a poster advertising your business.

3. When you are asked by the candidates to take a poll, make sure you understand what they want to find out from your survey.

4. Decide who you will survey for your poll and what questions you will ask.

5. Interview voters and analyze your results.

6. Make a graph showing your poll results.

7. Present your findings to the people who hired you to do the poll and share your poll results with the television reporters.

 **Activity Card**

Television Reporters

1. Make up a call name and number for your television station.

2. Decide which reporters will cover each campaign.

3. Begin to plan a 4- or 5-minute long Political News Update Show for your television station. The show can include campaign news, interviews with candidates, editorials by reporters or guest editorials, interviews with Election Board members, interviews with pollsters, and reports on survey results.

4. Talk with your teacher to find out where and when your show will be, whether it will be live or recorded, and how often it will be on the air.

5. Attend all speeches, press conferences, rallies, and other events given by candidates. Always bring a list of questions to ask candidates.

6. Help the candidates and their campaign staffs decide when their political ads will appear—before, during, or after your station's news show.

7. Make public service announcements reminding people to register and vote.

8. On Election Day, get the results of the election from the Election Board and report them on your news show.

Candidates, Campaigns & Elections 4th Ed © 2007 by Scher & Johnson, Scholastic Teaching Resources, page 77

Name _____

2008 Election Wrap-Up: Northeast

The race is run and now it's time to name the winners and losers.

	STATE	DEMOCRAT	REPUBLICAN	WINNER	% OF VOTE FOR WINNER
Electing a Governor	Delaware				
	New Hampshire				
	Vermont				
	Total Elections Won				
Electing a Senator	Delaware				
	New Hampshire				
	New Jersey				
	Maine				
	Massachusetts				
	Rhode Island				
	Total Elections Won				

Which political party added or lost seats in congress? _____

Name _____

2008 Election Wrap-Up: Midwest

The race is run and now it's time to name the winners and losers.

	STATE	DEMOCRAT	REPUBLICAN	WINNER	% OF VOTE FOR WINNER
Electing a Governor	Indiana				
	Missouri				
	North Dakota				
	Total Elections Won				
Electing a Senator	Illinois				
	Iowa				
	Kansas				
	Michigan				
	Minnesota				
	Nebraska				
	South Dakota				
	Total Elections Won				

Which political party added or lost seats in congress? _____

 **Name** _____

2008 Election Wrap-Up: Southeast

The race is run and now it's time to name the winners and losers.

	STATE	DEMOCRAT	REPUBLICAN	WINNER	% OF VOTE FOR WINNER
Electing a Governor	North Carolina				
	West Virginia				
	Total Elections Won				
Electing a Senator	Alabama				
	Arkansas				
	Georgia				
	Kentucky				
	Louisiana				
	Mississippi				
	North Carolina				
	South Carolina				
	Tennessee				
	Virginia				
	West Virginia				
	Total Elections Won				

Which political party added or lost seats in congress? _____

- -

 **Name** _____

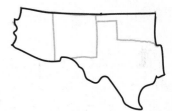

2008 Election Wrap-Up: Southwest

The race is run and now it's time to name the winners and losers.

	STATE	DEMOCRAT	REPUBLICAN	WINNER	% OF VOTE FOR WINNER
Electing a Governor	None				
Electing a Senator	New Mexico				
	Oklahoma				
	Texas				
	Total Elections Won				

Which political party added or lost seats in congress? _____

Name _____

2008 Election Wrap-Up: West

The race is run and now it's time to name the winners and losers.

	STATE	DEMOCRAT	REPUBLICAN	WINNER	% OF VOTE FOR WINNER
Electing a Governor	Montana				
	Utah				
	Washington				
Total Elections Won					
Electing a Senator	Alaska				
	Colorado				
	Idaho				
	Montana				
	Oregon				
	Wyoming				
Total Elections Won					

Which political party added or lost seats in congress? _____

- -

 Name _____

2008 Election Wrap-Up: My State

For many people, the most exciting races are the ones in their own backyard. Not every state or local official is up for reelection every election year. Although the Internet is a good place to research state and national elections, often the best place to find information on local elections is the local newspaper or local television news.

ELECTION HELD	POSITION	PARTY		WINNER
❏ YES ❏ NO	U.S. President	❏ DEMOCRAT	❏ REPUBLICAN	_____
❏ YES ❏ NO	Governor	❏ DEMOCRAT	❏ REPUBLICAN	_____
❏ YES ❏ NO	U.S. Senator	❏ DEMOCRAT	❏ REPUBLICAN	_____
❏ YES ❏ NO	U.S. Representative (My district: _____)	❏ DEMOCRAT	❏ REPUBLICAN	_____
❏ YES ❏ NO	State Senator (My district: _____)	❏ DEMOCRAT	❏ REPUBLICAN	_____
❏ YES ❏ NO	Mayor	❏ DEMOCRAT	❏ REPUBLICAN	_____